One-Step Financial Success

Implementing This One Step Will Take Away
All Your Financial Worries Forever!

Mark A. Schlossberg CLU

Copyright © 2019 Mark A. Schlossberg CLU
All rights reserved
First Edition

PAGE PUBLISHING, INC.
Conneaut Lake, PA

First originally published by Page Publishing 2019

ISBN 978-1-64628-589-1 (pbk)
ISBN 978-1-64628-590-7 (digital)

Printed in the United States of America

Disclaimers

This book was written to give general financial advice and not specific advice to each individual client. While every effort was made to make sure everything is accurate and up to date as possible, because of the changing dynamics of the financial industry and tax laws, some concepts in this book may become obsolete or maybe not applicable at all. Any errors whether by omission or commission are accidental. The author and publisher assume no responsibility for adverse consequences that may arise as a result of a client implementing the plans and concepts described in this book. As always for tax, legal, and financial advice, please consult the appropriate professional. Also please note that the author and publisher make no guarantees as to the success that one person achieves under this plan or if any success is achieved at all. While this book was written based upon the concepts, ideas, and financial vehicles of the American financial system, there are many jurisdictions that offer similar plans and financial vehicles (with possible small differences) to their residents. The ideas and concepts the author has outlined in *One-Step Financial Success* will work just as well within these jurisdictions, but the author urges readers to seek the advice of the appropriate professionals. Names of clients and prospective clients mentioned in the book were changed to protect the identity of these clients. However, this wasn't done for the author's family members. Reproduction of any part of this book, whether electronically or otherwise, without the written consent of the author and publisher is prohibited. Violators can be subjected to civil or criminal penalties.

This book is dedicated to all of you who are frustrated at the fact that no matter what you do, it seems that you struggle to get ahead financially. To all of you who want an "easy" method to tilt the odds in your favor financially. This book is for you.

Contents

Introduction 9

The Ideal Life 13
The Second Worst Mistake We Make 15
College Funding 18
Retirement Planning 24
Living Retired 36
The Solution (Ta-da!) 39
College Funding: The Solution 49
Retirement Funding: The Solution 52
Living Retired: The Solution 58

Acknowledgments 77
Notes 79

Introduction

How to Read This Book

John and Robin were best friends in high school. They would always go to the movies to enjoy a large half-meat-and-half-veggie pizza together after going to the movies to view whatever was the most-talked-about must-see movie at that time. They would always be seen studying together, and it was paying off, as they both kept straight As. Both graduated from high school with straight-A averages. John was accepted to Brown University, and Robin was accepted to Cornell University. They would both attend these respective schools.

John and Robin would receive some scholarship money but not enough to pay the full large tuition bill, which at that time, was estimated to be about $38,000 per year for each school. This, mind you, was just for tuition. This did not consider costs for room, board, books, etc. No worries, though, because both sets of parents were very financially savvy. Both mothers were teachers in the public school system. John's father was a cardiologist working long hours between his work at Baptist Hospital and his very successful practice. Robin's father was a very successful contractor with an extremely affluent clientele. Both sets of parents had saved whatever money they could in different retirement plans, and both sets of parents had nice pensions to live on throughout retirement. Both had large life insurance policies designed to leave large financial legacies to John and Robin when they died, so both sets of parents were able to bear the financial burdens for their children's education.

Just as important are the financial lessons both children would learn as far as their life in college was concerned. John and Robin dated other people, but they would telephone each other two, maybe three times a week or (yes, this was in the days before Facebook, Skype, etc.) they would spend time when they went home for holiday breaks, but most of the time, they would both burn the midnight oil and bury their heads in books. It would pay off, though, as both continued to receive straight-A grades, and both would graduate magna cum laude. As luck and fate would have it, John and Robin were accepted to the prestigious John Hopkins medical school. They were thrilled because now they could endure all the education and stress together. Eventually, they did marry each other. John followed his father's footsteps, worked at Baptist Hospital, and had a successful cardiology practice. Robin would be a successful pulmonologist in her own right, and she would spend long hours between working at Saint Bernard's hospital and her thriving practice. They bought a 5,000-square-foot English-style Tudor home with a stucco face and a circular drive in a very upscale part of the neighborhood. John and Robin would have two beautiful daughters named Gina and Rachel. This means they would have arguments about the type of automobile they would drive. John wanted a cool-looking sports sedan, but Robin would politely but firmly explain to John that he was a family man and that he needed to have a large SUV for themselves, the children, and various parents.

They were financially succeeding at this point, and, for the most part, they, like their parents, had lived generally modestly. They did not eat out often or take extravagant vacations, so to "compromise," they bought an Alfa Romeo for John and a large GMC Yukon SUV to satisfy both John's and Robin's automobile ownership wishes. John and Robin saved and invested their money in their own retirement plans, and they started separate college funds early, as soon as the children were born. With this plan, they could withdraw their money tax-free, and, possibly, they could qualify for a scholarship for private college education for their children This would not be a scholarship based on financial need or academic success but based on the fact that they simply did their part in saving for Gina's and Rachel's education. The funds in this plan would not need to be counted or reported to the colleges, and as a result, they would not be used against them if they were to apply for financial aid. John and Robin also had the foresight to plan long-term for the eventual situation when they would not be around for the children anymore. They realized that taxes would be due because of the income generated from their qualified plans. The children would not have to pay these taxes out of their pockets. During their retirement, John and Robin were able to travel the world, give generously to their house of worship and to various other charities, and spend large amounts of time with their grandchildren and their hobbies. Robin took art classes to learn how to paint, and John would be active in his grandchild's Little League and as a trustee of his house of worship. They also took pride in the fact that Gina and Rachel learned these financial lessons that their parents had taught them and that their children would have so much success in their lives also.

The Ideal Life

Now that we had enjoyed living life vicariously through our fictional characters, John and Robin, let's reflect on our own lives for a minute to ask ourselves this simple question, and that is "What do we want?" At least in a financial sense, the journey of life that John and Robin were living seems ideal, and it is. When I ask my clients what they want, some say, "I want to upgrade or downsize our home" or "I would like a fancier car." Some say they want to retire comfortably and leave a legacy to their children. I believe that these wants are just a small part of living an ideal life, and there is nothing wrong with wanting these things. However, there will be obstacles toward achieving this ideal life. Some caused by us, and some by outside forces. As a result, we will make some very critical mistakes which will prevent us from living the ideal financial life or the type of life that John and Robin were living.

Call me crazy or a cockeyed idealist, but I believe we deserve, and, even by necessity, we must have this type of life if we want to enjoy it and be most fulfilled. I believe there is one solution that when implemented, can cut through these obstacles and take us to where we need to go financially.

This book will be your handy guide toward implementing this solution. I believe there are three main areas in which we make some serious financial mistakes. They are in college (education) funding, retirement planning, and retired living. I will discuss the mistakes we are making in this order because in most cases, as we travel through life, this is the order of the stages we encounter. With this book, I will engage your laugh muscles, entertain, and educate, but most importantly, this will be an unapologetic call to action. Unfortunately, only you with a little help—and that is where we come in—can take responsibility for making sure you keep and not needlessly give away money that you have worked so hard to accumulate and save.

I will get personal with the mistakes I have made, and you will get to know members of my family very well. This book is written in a very direct, down-to-earth, and in-your-face style, but I will use copious amounts of humor to hopefully inspire you to take actions to make sure that you are living your ideal life. This may not be the most polished book on financial planning you will ever read, but I promise you I am only concerned about your financial welfare. Other entities are concerned about themselves. Someone should look after us. After twenty-nine years of making this my life's calling, I need not worry about proper image anyway. Enough of this dribble, and let's get on with the meat of this book.

The Second Worst Mistake We Make

As I left off the last chapter, we will go over the mistakes that we make in college funding, retirement planning, and retired living in that order because, again, this is the order of events that happen in the lives of most people. You might be thinking this is an odd title for the section, but in my younger days, before the responsibilities of life hit me, I was an avid bowler. I bowled in many leagues in my day, and the way we organized our team lineup is that we put our second-best bowler first, as he was supposed to be the person who would set a positive tone for us with a good start. We felt that if he started off well, we, as a team, were most likely to keep it up. So in my humble opinion, the second worst mistake we make is that we listen too much to other people's advice, opinions, etc. that it discourages us to think and act for ourselves. We do this because it is ingrained in us to be popular, to not rock the boat, or, dare I say, "be corporate," for those who work as employees in corporate America. We are also afraid of the "I told you so" or the harsh ridicule from other people when things don't work the way it should.

There are several problems with this. The first is that we listen to friends, coworkers, or other people we know. These people have well-meaning intentions, and they mean no harm for us, but they may not be necessarily financial experts. Every person is unique and different, just like your fingerprint, so what may be good for one family unit or person might not be for another family unit or person. We try to get advice from our friendly neighborhood financial television personality, but, again, these people are generally well-intentioned, but please understand their job is to entertain, and their success is not necessarily driven by your financial success but by their television ratings. They're unlike rock stars and athletes whose entertainment success hinges on their audience enjoying a show or a game, and there probably will not be a tremendous lifetime impact, good or bad. Listening to these TV financial gurus may not prove to be the wisest financial decision you can make. In fact, it may prove to be very costly because this advice deals directly with how one should use their monetary resources. Most of them have some general knowledge about the specific items they are talking about, they don't know the specifics of your financial situation.

I will give you a personal example of this: my mother, whom I will refer to also later. She used to watch the shopping show QVC. One of the occasional hosts/vendors at that time was a very famous female financial advisor. She was proposing to the TV audience to purchase long-term care insurance, a good piece of advice where appropriate, but the problem that I had was that she was advising the TV audience to purchase this insurance from only one insurance carrier. This, of course, limited the audience to purchase policies and accompanying options of only this one company with obviously no deviation. Not all the advice was awful, please understand, but one would question her objectivity and her motives to work only with this one carrier. Anyway, my mother, out of curiosity, did call the recommended phone number. The longest duration policy they offered was for a benefit period of five years. This was unacceptable to my mother because she wanted a lifetime benefit plan. Because I was in the financial services business, she knew she could purchase that type of plan. What about people who don't have that type of knowledge or connection? They would have to settle for the smaller benefit-paying policy if they did not want that. This could possibly lead to some financial complications later on, and I will briefly touch on them later in the book.

Having said all this, why should I ask you to listen to little old me? Who am I to deserve your attention? I have made financial services my life's calling for over twenty-nine years. I have seen my prospective clients and regular clients make these critical mistakes. On a personal level, growing up the oldest of four boys with a single mother, no father, and no money (and I mean having-to-eat-cereal-and-milk-with-a-fork no money, I mean people-breaking-into-my-house-to-leave-things-in my-house no money), I had always wanted to make sure that in my adult life, I would help people become better off financially than I was. That is why I made this my life's calling. I have also made some of these mistakes myself. I can tell you I am not concerned with how much product I move, but I want to help as many people live the type of life that John and Robin from earlier were living. I want to see people live in a financial world where mistakes are minimized or even eliminated.

Before we leave this topic, I want to bring us back to 1997 and hope that I can drive home the point of thinking for yourself and not following the crowd. In 1997, we all remember the Heaven's Gate cult. All of America was captivated by them. I am only going to give you a very brief summary of what happened. They believed that the Earth would be destroyed because of all of the evil on it. They would be transported to a new and better homeland. Their leader saw a shooting star, and he believed that this was the time to leave, so each member ingested a mixture of vodka, applesauce, and poison. They put plastic bags around their heads after ingesting this to induce asphyxiation. Basically, this was a murder-suicide of thirty-nine people. So what's the point of bringing this up? The point is, logically, who would possibly believe that you could travel on a shooting star to reach a better, heavenly place and take your life to do it? But no one dared to be different and say, "This is ridiculous, and I am not ending my life, and I'm leaving," and everyone felt that they needed to conform and be popular, but in doing so, it would cost them their lives. This is extreme, but, seriously, you cannot rely on other people to advise you on your financial situation, and your decisions should be based on your personal situation and yours alone. Don't worry! I will be harping on this point. You will be "lovingly hating me" all through the book because it is that important. Does that sound exciting?

College Funding

Now, our first big financial milestone I want to dig into is college funding. According to The Institute for College Access and Success (TICAS) in 2017, 65% of graduating seniors who had graduated from public and nonprofit private colleges had student debt. These borrowers hold an average of $28,650 in tuition. Tuition prices at universities for the class of 2034 will reach $110,432 per year if rates continue to rise as they have over the last three decades. This is outrageous! Here I thought that you wouldn't have to pay too much to learn that $X = 2$ for the equation $2 + X = 4$, but this is amazing. How come approximately two out of three graduating seniors have so much debt that these students start out right out after graduation with negative financial net worth or, in English, "owing a whole lot of bread" (or for all of my fellow *Sopranos* fans, a lot of boxes of ziti)? Well, I can tell you at least one nonfinancial reason. It is that there is still so much emphasis today on obtaining a college degree. After all, that's where the good jobs are, or so we've been told. People, though, are not saving enough for this important milestone or not saving money properly, and I will outline some of the key mistakes now.

Thinking You Are Too Young or Affluent to Worry about Saving for Your Children's Education?

First, I want to congratulate you if you are one of the few who have accumulated enough funds be considered extremely financially secure. I know that for most of you, it took years of hard work, toil, and using your talents wisely. Here, though, is where the problem may arise in terms of saving for and paying for college. Although you may be able to pay for education yourself, unless your assets are in cash or somehow liquid, you will probably have to sell assets. That means generating potentially large outrageous tax payments. You know our government loves this. You shouldn't have to. I will discuss in great detail my hatred of the injustices of our own tax system throughout the book.

Also keep in mind we mentioned earlier that if you have multiple children or graduate schools to finance, it gets much harder to sell assets quickly. Eventually, there may come a point where you simply don't have the assets to sell.

As far as being too young is concerned, that is the best time, of course, to start saving for college because you will have the advantage of time. The best time to accumulate the funds to reach the amount you will need to pay for college is when the children are young. You need the time for interest to accumulate on your funds to reach the tuition funding goals. The longer you wait—of course, common sense would dictate—the harder it will be to accumulate the funds you will need at the specific time to pay the college tuition. And for those of you who are on the affluent end of the financial spectrum—in some circumstances, as I will discuss also later in the book—you may be able to receive a scholarship just for saving money for college. So, wouldn't it be nice for somebody to actually give you something for a change instead of having everybody ask you for things because you are so financially fortunate? Also, as I will bring up later with the planning you will employ after reading the book, the amount of funds that you accumulate will not be used to count adversely toward receiving financial aid for your children's education.

Taking out Big Loans to Pay for Education Funding

I always love it when people say that student loans are a good way to pay for college. This statement is not necessarily made by experts, but it is made by general ordinary people. Bull cookies, in my opinion. Unless the graduate starts earning enough income to pay the loans right away, or at the very least, within six months after graduation, the vicious cycle begins. As soon as the graduate starts missing payments, lenders advise the credit bureaus. Potential employers look at the credit reports on these prospective employees, and would-be employers take a pass on hiring them. This, most of the time, is generally the main reason that our otherwise talented graduates can't find employment right away. More time goes by with more missed payments with accompanying interest and penalties added. ("Why not have this debt grow bigger than my waistline?") This leads to more employment search rejection, and the whole mess gets bigger and bigger. After a while, these graduates are labeled as irresponsible and, dare I say, deadbeats, and never mind all this emotional drain and self-respect theft they have to go through.

With all this technology we have, you can write a bad check, and everyone knows about it. James Kvaal, president of TICAS, said, "We need to invest more in student aid and in college to reduce students' need to borrow and make their loans easier to pay." To that I say, "Duh! Thank you, Mr. Kvaal." If you think our government or the lenders are going to rush to reform that system, you're wasting your time waiting. They prefer not to lose that potential interest income they will receive from these loans and programs, or in the case of our government, they prefer to shift the costs and expenses of funding tertiary education to us. Fear not, my friends. With a little advance planning, you can beat the system. Read on!

Using Your Retirement Plan to Pay for Your Children's Education

This gem is another biggie regarding mistakes in college funding. Why? One reason is that it is a way to access a potentially large sum of money in a very short period. Most of the time, if a family needs to access their money from their retirement plan, it is, to put it bluntly, the result of either rotten or no planning at all.

One time, one of my husband and wife clients, James and Tamara, had a son starting college named David. He was about to start attending a prestigious university. The tuition for the first year at this university was approximately $18,500. It would be reasonable to assume that this tuition would stay the same throughout David's four years in the best-case scenario. One thing for sure was that the tuition would not decrease. James and Tamara were new clients for me. At the time they paid for the $18,500 tuition from their retirement plans, they were in the 28% federal tax bracket with a state tax at 9%, and both clients were under the age of fifty-nine and a half years old. So, between the taxes and the early withdrawal penalty, they had to withdraw $38,533.75 from one of the retirement plans. Who, in their right minds, would withdraw more than double the required money they needed to pay a college tuition? Especially to pay taxes and penalties to boot? This is what happens without proper planning. Keep in mind that this is just for tuition and not for the other expenses like room, board, meals, etc. Theoretically, James and Tamara would have to do this three more times for the other years of school, and potentially, James and Tamara would more than likely have to do this with their high school-age son, Michael, when he was ready for college. Unfortunately, what happened to James and Tamara happens with families all over the US. I also imagine this also happens anywhere else where one can invest in similar types of employer plans. As you can imagine, our government is not going to be in any rush to discourage such behavior and lose all that newfound tax money. Your objective should be, obviously, to want to keep more of your money, and these withdrawals are not the way to go.

Using Your Home as an ATM

I will give everyone a small break now because I will make this one short and sweet. I see too many people leverage their home with debt to pay education expenses. Some people have multiple mortgages, home equity loans, etc. In effect, they are building and living in a prison. Albeit a very nice prison but still one, nonetheless. The Grand Canyon will be fully complete before you will have built enough substantial equity to make a sale of your home more profitable.

Failing to Insure Your Children's Education Fund

Let me ask everyone a question. If we assume that you had no legal constraints and you had free will entirely, if you lived in a million-dollar mansion or drove a Maserati, would you insure it against the risk of fire, accident, elephant stampede, etc.? Or would you let the force be with you and bet nothing will ever happen but pay all the expenses to repair or replace your home or car if it did? The answer generally would be "Of course, we would insure our home and our car. I am not an idiot!" Most people, or I should say the vast majority, have health insurance to protect themselves from a lengthy hospital stay or at least to defray the cost of doctor visits and pharmaceuticals. Most people have some sort of life insurance, at the very least, to secure some multiple of their income and to have family members pay off their final expense debt upon their death. Most people, however, do not insure their children's education expenses. I have to say that this will probably be your only large expense ever other than your home. When I recommend purchasing insurance to cover this expense, however, people look at me as if I'm telling them that London is the capital of France. If you could learn how to ensure that these funds would be paid upon your death, disability, or critical illness, and it would only cost you pennies on the dollar, wouldn't that be something that you would love to learn about? Later on, we will go over the solution to this college funding faux pas. I hope I'm spelling that right. I'm rusty with my French.

Putting It All Together

What does all of this mean? What it means is that although our intentions are good and that based on our financial situation, we are doing the best we can, we are still trying to access money we have no right to access yet or, an even more dangerous proposition, try to use money that we simply do not have. This is costing us thousands upon thousands of dollars and hurting us financially. Banks, our US government, colleges, and universities are benefiting *big-time* from our misfortune. They want to encourage us to keep on engaging in these financial exercises that only lead to our financial hardship. They want *more of your money*. What is really horrible about this situation is that most families have to execute some of the aforementioned strategies over and over again for multiple years and with multiple children and possibly other schools, like graduate school. Let's stop this madness and execute a better plan. We will talk about this plan soon enough.

Retirement Planning

Defined Benefit Plans vs. Defined Contribution Plans

Now we are going to discuss the next big financial milestone that most people will experience. And this is retirement planning. Now I will tell you this. I am not going to get into strategies of picking stocks or timing the market or what mutual funds some people should get, buy, and hold, or sell, blah, blah, blah. I'm going to leave that discussion for other books and people who are smarter than I am. What I'm going to discuss now in this book are the different problems that we will experience in our saving for retirement. Part of the problem in retirement planning is that people are generally investing in one type of retirement plan.

What we have are two types of retirement plan structures you can invest in. The first plan is called a defined benefit plan. In a defined benefit plan, you can predict the specific financial amount you can accumulate with the plan at a certain time in your life. For example, when you turn sixty-five, your account will hold $500,000. In this way, you can tell which is the right investment plan to use and the right amount to invest so you can achieve your financial goal. A great example of these type of plans are the pension plans that companies used to offer their employees. The way these plans worked was that the company would contribute various amounts of money over time to deliver a promised benefit. Yes, the employer took full responsibility in investing for the employee and made all of the decisions. The employees did not have to worry about a thing. That promised benefit was passed on to the employees when they retired. So, in the days where people used to receive pensions, an employee was guaranteed a certain amount of money per month or year for the rest of his life, and he didn't have to worry about that. That didn't mean that the employee was prohibited to invest in another plan on his own so he can take a certain amount of money monthly for the rest of his and his family's life.

Let me give you a nonfinancial example of a defined benefit plan. A defined benefit plan is like taking a trip from New York to Los Angeles. You know you can get there in a variety of ways—by plane, by car, by bus, by camel, hitchhike on the back of a crocodile, or any other combination of ways you want—but you know that the goal is to reach Los Angeles, and you know you will absolutely do so with no worries. I believe that more people—no, I want to change that to everybody—should be investing along the lines of looking for defined benefit plans to invest in because at least, you know no matter what the conditions are, you will always receive the amount that you had set as a financial goal.

The other type of plan is called a defined contribution plan. Essentially, a defined contribution plan is a plan where you set aside a fixed amount or a fixed percentage or some other fixed formula of money per month or per year or whatever, and you will have absolutely no idea about the amount of the fund you will have accumulated at the specified time you desire. Or simply put, you will not know what you're going to have in the end. This is a plan that relies on investment strategy—each investor's financial skill and investment ability—and outside forces that one can't control. However, these forces certainly control the investment results. These are your 401(k) plans or any other another tax-qualified plans that employers offer.

A typical defined contribution plan will have wording such as this: "We will contribute 50¢ for every dollar you contribute to our plan for a maximum of 3% of your salary." That means you will need to contribute 6% of your salary for your employer to contribute 3%, as in this example. I will also give you a nonfinancial example of what a defined contribution plan is. This is the type of travel plan where you still want to travel from New York to Los Angeles, but now you have the following directions you must follow. You are told to travel by car 600 miles straight, then make a left, and travel another 300 miles. From there, this time, take a bus for 100 miles. Then go straight again for another 200 miles, and take another car for another 105 miles, and that's it. Will you be in Los Angeles after following this? I would say not because you will have to travel about 3,000 miles, but you were told to follow these directions. Now you are on your own to come up with the rest of the directions you need to travel to successfully reach Los Angeles.

Defined contribution plans seem to be the most prevalent plans that are implemented now, and these are the plans that most employers will offer instead of the old defined benefit pension plans.

If you go by this explanation that I had made above, it would seem a wonder why would anybody want to invest in a defined contribution plan if they're not sure what's going to happen with their money at a certain time or if they will have the required amount when they retire. The answer to this can be found in the question "Why do we have these plans in the first place?" The answer lies in the fact that corporations and our government "highly encourage" participation. In the good old days of corporate benefits, employers and companies used to offer pension plans as their retirement plan option. The idea was that you could work and toil for the same employer for twenty or thirty years or whatever, and when you decide to "hang it up," they would give you a nice party, a watch, a plaque, and a monthly income for the rest of your life and possibly the life of one, and only one, family member. A pension is a fancy word for monthly income for life. Unfortunately, in today's business climate, offering pensions are not practical. Workers are staying with an employer for much less time than the twenty or thirty years they used to stay. Sometimes they are leaving on their own for "better pastures," or they are leaving because employers are asking them to, but they are leaving much sooner than in the good old days. The loyalty is not there on either side. It is also very costly to administer a pension plan because as an employer, they are taking responsibility for providing the promised benefits. They need to make sure the correct amount is always invested even in the worst-case scenarios, and they need to pay actuaries and consultants to help them do this. It is not practical anymore to provide a pension plan, but employers still have a problem. They still need to attract and retain valuable, talented employees. They need to offer benefits to do that, and everybody wants retirement benefits. So, what is a company to do?

They offer your 401(k) plan. It is much less costly, and it shifts the responsibility to an employee to save for retirement. The employee now not only has to be skilled at his natural talent or the job that he is been hired to do, but also he must be very skilled at money management and in investing. There is no pressure here, right? Later in the book, I will show you a way to take care of your retirement without the skill you need to be a good money manager. That is why corporations encourage 401(k) plans. Why does the government encourage it? The answer—well, we will make it nice, short, and sweet—is taxes. Especially if you "don't follow the rules" and fall into their traps. With the fact that by 2020, 16.9% of Americans will be over sixty-five years old, and the national debt will be over $22 trillion as of 2019. The government needs to raise as much tax revenue as it can, and it might as well be at yours and your family's expense, so they think. These retirement plans have great potential to earn nice sums of money, and that is an ingredient that the government needs for their recipe for taking a lot of money through taxes. They can't wait.

Your Two Basic Enemies in Retirement Planning

If we were to look up the word *enemy* in the dictionary, the definition of enemy would be someone who opposes or wishes harm to you. In this book, there are two specific enemies that I am going to address. The first one is taxation from the government via the IRS and states, etc. Basically, what they are saying through their taxation policies is that you have worked very hard to accumulate and save all of this money that you have in your retirement plans, so it is only fair that we take as much of it as we want. After all, why should you have any of it? How do they do this? By hoping you will fall into their built-in traps by mistake and by causing taxable events so they can take away your money, and lots of it are through taxes, penalties, etc. The second enemy that you need to watch out for is death. This is a very overlooked and underplanned for area that the government hopes to use to snare innocent people into their money trap. After all—I could say this with absolute certainty—each of us will have one death. If you can execute the plan that I'm going to show you later on in the book, you will minimize the impact of these taxes so that your family and even you can keep more of the money that you have accumulated.

I want to clarify something before I move on, though. I absolutely believe that all Americans need to pay their fair share of taxes. I emphasize the word *fair* because I believe that once you trigger a taxable event, you do need to pay the resulting tax. But when you or your family must lose 50% or more of your tax-qualified plan assets to the government, that does not seem fair. With this book, I am not going to show you how to avoid paying your taxes but how you will replace the money you will pay in taxes so that it appears as if you or your family will not be paying these taxes out of your pocket. In this case, everyone will be happy. The government gets paid quickly, and the family has all the money it deserves. But, again, keep in mind that only you with a little help—and that's where I come in—can take responsibility for making sure that you keep and not needlessly give away money that you have worked so hard to accumulate and save.

Before we go further, I just want to clarify something else. In this book, I will use the term *401(k) plan* for the sake of simplicity and brevity, but this book also applies if you have an IRA; a TSA, which is a tax-sheltered annuity; or any other tax-qualified plan. In some cases, you might not need to have any tax-qualified plan at all. This can apply to anyone who has been saving for retirement. There are many traps associated with a 401(k) plan. Having said that, I am not against anyone contributing to these plans so long as the employer offers to match the contribution that you make to his plan. This is free money. My feeling is that you should only contribute an amount that would maximize the "free money" that your employer will give. To summarize, for a tax-qualified plan, the maximum you should contribute should be the amount that would generate the maximum employer contribution because any other contribution will create taxable money. If at present you are contributing more than this maximum, this book will reveal the potential dangers of doing so and, more importantly, will show you a better way to invest the money safely in terms of minimizing potential taxes.

Let's Talk about Death

Now I want to address the next biggest enemy. That is your death. In my twenty-nine plus years of making my life's calling in the financial service industry, I can honestly say that advising people to financially prepare for their death is one of the more difficult things to do. Why is that? I feel that there are two main reasons for this. The first is that it is too morbid to think about it, and the second is that it requires inertia to take the steps to financially plan for it. I will briefly examine these reasons in more detail.

Everyone knows about the Titanic. When this ship was built, it was supposed to be the ship that couldn't sink. It was supposed to be indestructible. Why didn't it reach its intended destination? It hit an iceberg. Now I will ask, *Would it have been too morbid for the builders to ask how could this ship withstand a deadly collision?* Most people would not think that morbid at all. Most people would feel that it was necessary to ask this and an exercise in malpractice if they didn't. This is called planning. Evidently, the builders of the Titanic did not do a wonderful job planning for this scenario because we all know what happened to the Titanic. The unsinkable ship sunk, and many lives were lost. I do not want to beat a dead mule, but the government would like to see you do this type of bad planning regarding your retirement plans because a penny saved is a penny earned for them.

The second reason for not planning for death is good old lack of inertia, or in practical terms, we call it procrastination. If I remember my high school and college physics courses correctly, inertia can be described as the energy needed to put an object in motion. I failed my college course miserably. As a funny aside, I knew that studying physics was not something I should do. On my very first exam in college, I achieved a 17% score. The professor wrote on my exam paperwork, "Hopeless, advised to withdraw." Needless to say, I took her advice.

In this case, the object that should be put in motion is planning for your death through retirement plans. I know it is not exciting necessarily to plan for other people. After all, "I won't be around, so I'm just giving other people money so they can enjoy it." This is a statement that I have heard more times than I can count. Please don't misunderstand. These people have good intentions, but "now I'm towing my car; there's a hole in the roof. / My possessions are causing me suspicion, but there's no proof." (I'm sorry for that Crowded House reference.) With other things that need your attention and your money, it is very easy to put planning your finances on the back burner. But, again, Uncle Sam is patiently waiting on the horizon, and he hopes you never get around to planning the way you're supposed to. I have a deep personal connection with this inertia that I will share in a few more minutes. So why have I gone through all this trouble for us to talk about this? Good question and one I will answer now. If you believe nothing else from me as you read this book, you need to know this one fact, and eat, breathe, and live it. That is *the worst place to have your money upon your death is in a tax-qualified plan!*

Why is this the case? It all depends upon who is to receive the money upon your death. If the money is left to a spouse, there is no taxable event because of the spousal deduction. Bear in mind that it is not an avoidance of tax but merely a deferral of taxes. This is only a setup for the sonic boom that will happen later. If the money is to be left to a living nonspouse beneficiary (or beneficiaries), this money will be taxed as regular income according to its corresponding tax bracket. Here are the federal tax brackets for 2019.

ONE-STEP FINANCIAL SUCCESS

Rate	Unmarried individuals Income over:	Married, filing jointly Income over:	Head of household Income over:
0%	$0	$0	$0
12%	$9,700	$19,400	$13,850
22%	$39,475	$78,950	$52,850
24%	$84,200	$168,400	$84,200
32%	$160,725	$321,450	$160,700
35%	$204,100	$408,200	$204,100
37%	$510,300	$612,350	$510,300

It is easy to see that it would not be that difficult to accumulate $200,000, $300,000, or even the top bracket rate of $612,350 for married couples filing jointly or $510,300, for a person filing single as an unmarried person. The worst part of this is that there are no substantial deductions from this inherited income that you can take to reduce the tax burden and thus receive a very high income tax bill that Uncle Sam will gladly send you. I want to give you a personal example of this. My mother taught junior high school history (or what we used to call social studies) for over twenty years. I would advise my mother on her financial situation periodically even if she needed other people to implement the recommended plan.

Now I will digress. For all of you readers who had parents complain that you did not listen to them, believe it or not, a lot of times, this role reverses, and they don't listen to you. My mother had accumulated over $210,000 approximately in her TSA (Tax-Sheltered Annuity) plan. I had approached her many times about this very subject of the taxes that we, as her children, would pay up on her demise because of the TSA distribution. My mother procrastinated in implementing a tax protection plan regarding this. I can imagine, though, her thinking might have been, "Well, yeah, Mark, you know-it-all. After I changed your diapers for many years, and through a lot of your school years, your grades were lower than…" You get the idea.

I was not aggressive enough to make her prioritize taking the action needed to solve this problem. Remember, I mentioned earlier in this book my own lapse in judgment about overcoming the inertia to act. This is it.

My mother died in 2005. My three brothers and I were all very close. In 2006, we received our distribution, and instead of receiving around $200,000, because of these taxes, we had received only about $95,000 in total. Each of us received roughly $24,000, less than half the balance she had accumulated.

For those of you who want the twenty-ounce T-bone steak of an example, enjoy this. In the late 1990s, I had two parents as my clients named Tom and Dana, and they had three adult children: Michael, Lisa, and Ilana. Tom was a bank's regional vice president, and Dana was a science teacher in high school. Both had tax-qualified plans at work, and both contributed about 15% of their salary to their plans. As we established early in this book, this was no good because, essentially, you're accumulating taxable money. They lived modestly and comfortably. Very few vacations, fancy dinners, or luxury items. Tom died in 1999 and accumulated $2,010,950 in his plan. This money was left to Dana, and because of the spousal deduction, there were no taxes to pay by any family member. So far so good. Dana had accumulated $618,417 in her own retirement plan, and by the time of her death two years later, as a result, Michael, Lisa, and Ilana would divide retirement plan assets of $3,229,367. This means that each child would receive a total of $976,455. Please understand, all these children were all college-educated and all had received master's degrees, so they were not naive enough to believe that taxes would not have to be paid on this amount. They just were not expecting that they had to pay what they ended up paying. After federal and state income taxes and the estate taxes, only $466,519 of the original $3,229,367 was left. Each child received roughly over $160,000, approximately 85% of their parent's retirement plans eliminated through taxation.

I can't stress enough what these two examples are showing. They are showing that with immediate action to implement this planning solution, my brothers and I would have paid the $115,000 tax and still have the $115,000. Michael, Lisa and Ilana would have paid the taxes resulting from the $976,000 inheritance and still have the $976,000.

Most of my colleagues' advice to their clients focus on what they should do with their retirement plans and how they can minimize taxation upon taking distributions from their plans. That is what they should do. I provide my clientele such advice, but—and this is a big *but*—they mostly are providing advice for what you should do while you are alive. Because of the mistakes I made with my mother's retirement plan, I am taking this one step further, and I want to make sure that your family receives all the money they are entitled to and that they can pay all the tax they need to. As an aside, this has caused a little bit of a strain in my relationship with my brothers because I was probably the most emotionally close to my mother. I was also the oldest, and professionally, I should have known better.

One thing I will mention is estate taxes. These taxes are also called death taxes or inheritance taxes. They are based not on income but on the aggregate of assets that are passed down. Even some advisers make the mistake of believing that death taxes are dead, but I am sorry to say it is alive and well. But there is some good news here. This tax has a filing threshold. That means that there is a minimum amount of assets that you need to have before you need to pay this tax. In 2018 and for the foreseeable future, that amount is over $11 million. So, for most people now, they probably do not have to worry about that as much. But just as the government can raise the income tax rates, they can also lower the filing threshold for a estate tax. Remember the example of Tom and Dana. When Dana died in 2001, the filing threshold for a estate taxation was only $675,000; meaning if more than $675,000 was passed down as inheritance, that excess amount was taxed. Even then it was not difficult to reach this threshold.

The point is *Who knows what the future for any taxation ruling holds?* Remember, this is a government who needs to raise a lot of revenue very quickly while our national debt is, again, at about $22 trillion and climbing. There is over $5 trillion in retirement plans money that can be taxed. I know by now you are saying to yourselves,

"Thanks, Mark. I want to help my family, but there's got to be something in it for me too." There is, and I like to call this the bonus section of my book. For starters, with these plans, there is great potential to earn tax-free money. If you remember on a couple of occasions, I had mentioned that you should only contribute to your plan enough for you to receive the maximum free money your employer will give you in his tax-qualified plan. If you invest any more than this, the plan's gain is taxable, subject to the distribution rules of the plan that most people know about. Also, your money will be imprisoned in the plan because of the harsh penalties for early withdrawal. Usually this is about 10% on top of the income tax that your distribution would generate. Yeah! Also, these plans are generally funded through equity securities (stocks and mutual funds), so now outside forces beyond your control determine how your plan will perform. You might need to try to adjust your investment strategy or take it on the chin (remember 2008). With our planning, you do not have to do too much. Just put in your predetermined investment all the time without fail, and that's the extent of the money management expertise you need. This money will accumulate tax-free, and no need to worry about money prison.

Also, just an aside, if you have young children, this is an effective way to save for college. Money you accumulate here will not be counted adversely by colleges or the government when the time comes to figure out financial aid. Think about that! For example, let's say your assets consist of a home and $500,000 accumulated in this plan we are advising you to invest your money in, and both parents' salary incomes total $150,000 annually. Colleges and the federal government need only know about the income and the house. This $500,000 you have invested with our plan structure will be *your little secret*. How *awesome* is that! You can have significant assets and still get significant financial aid for education.

Another beautiful thing about this plan is that if you need long-term medical or nursing care or if you suffer a critical illness (for example, cancer, heart attack, stroke, etc.), this plan may be able to provide the funds you need to meet those expenses. This can be a financial lifesaver if that happens. Yes, I know that some people now think I have lost what is totally left of my mind. I will assure you now that the plan I will show you can be easily executed, and you will not have to worry about silly things like our trade policy in Singapore, or which countries are fighting with each other, or the price of soybeans in Guatemala, or some other outside factor that could determine how well or how poorly your qualified retirement plans and other equity security-based investments perform. The point is you can't control these outside factors; however, with the planning we recommend, you know it will succeed because you have total control. You will learn more about this as I continue explaining more in the book in the sections ahead.

Living Retired

This section is for those fortunate enough to be living through and enjoying their golden retirement years. Let me firstly congratulate you for reaching this wonderful milestone in your life. I also hope you are enjoying your retirement life in good health, and you are enjoying all your activities and your relationships. Regarding your financial situation, I do not believe there are too many major mistakes that are being made, but there are some, nonetheless. There are two that I want to elaborate on for this section.

Watch Your Assets

I will briefly touch on this here, but it is not really the focus of this book. But hey, what's another reminder among friends? I am referring to preserving and transferring assets to avoid losing them to our government in order to obtain Medicaid funding. Please remember that you must make your transfers at least five years earlier of applying for Medicaid. For example, if you are applying for Medicaid funding in May of 2019, asset transfers out of your name must have been completed by May of 2014 at the latest. In the old days, if the transfers were not made outside of this five-year window, the government would simply recount the assets in your name in order to determine Medicaid funding eligibility. It was as if the transfers had never happened. The problem was, of course, that no one could ever know if or when they would need long-term nursing care. So, essentially, you will gamble on when is the best date to transfer assets. Incredulously, at one point in some cases, they called it an illegal transfer, and that could theoretically subject you to a felony charge with prison time.

Three cheers to the government for this one, but luckily, in 1998, this was ruled unconstitutional. I guess the government assumed that most people had this magic crystal ball they could use to predict when they would become ill or when they would need nursing care. My hope for people in this situation is that they started planning for this early. I mean as soon as the thought of having to get rid of assets came to them. Hopefully, these people made transfers of assets early and even procured long-term care insurance policies, which are always a good bet. Even if you did not execute those solutions just mentioned, don't worry. The solution I will recommend will help pay for your long-term care needs, so have no fear!

Reverse Mortgages: Friend or Foe?

The other big concern I see for those living in retirement is the reverse mortgage phenomenon. In my opinion, a reverse mortgage is just like any other tool, financial or otherwise, that when used appropriately is outstanding and when not used properly is a disaster. Briefly, this is how it works.

To start, obviously, you must be a homeowner. You also must be sixty-two years of age or older to be named on the mortgage. The reverse mortgage is basically a slang name for what it really is. It is a home equity conversion mortgage. That means that it takes the equity built up in your home over time and converts it into cash that can be used now. You cannot physically lift your house and use it to pay for things. I don't care how physically strong and healthy you are; you cannot do that. In addition, it would be very difficult to slide your home through a credit card processing machine. Unfortunately, you need a middleman who would be your bank or lender to provide that cash for you. In return for that cash, the banker would place a mortgage lien on that home as collateral for this loan.

The reason it is referred to as a reverse mortgage is that you do not have to pay this loan back right away. It also does not have to be paid back by you. Also, lenders do not check everyone's credit score, assets, or income like they do for a traditional mortgage application.

The only items a lender looks at into is the age of the borrower and the available equity in the home. Usually, lenders will lend from 60% to 75% of the total value of the home based on the compared home values in the neighborhood (appraisals), and it all sounds wonderful, doesn't it? You get all the money that was doing nothing anyway, and you don't have to pay it back.

Awesome! One problem! The bank does not give this money as a gift. It gets paid back usually by the heirs when the last named spouse dies, and they need to pay back the whole amount within one year. Failure to do so means the bank will foreclose on the property just as they would do so for a regular mortgage default. So, in effect, it becomes a race.

Do the heirs race to sell a property for most likely less than fair market value because the property must be sold quickly? This is the better outcome because the heirs at least receive something. Or does the bank foreclose on the property, and the heirs do not receive anything? That's throwing away thousands of dollars of actual property.

The common seniors' misconception is that there is nothing that can be done about this nonsense, but we will disclose the solution to this. Not only will you avoid debt payments on your home, assuring family members that they do not have to sell the home upon your death and pay any money out of their pockets, you will also be able to leverage this equity in your home for a nice monthly income for your retirement years. Please read on!

The Solution (Ta-da!)

We Are Here

We are here! We are now at the point of our little book where will reveal this amazing planning tool that will help to alleviate and satisfy all these potential problems that we have spoken about during our little journey so far. Keep in mind one common theme that we have been talking about. We have been talking about different problems we could encounter should we die. We have been talking about potential solutions while we are alive and about situations we would encounter should we become sick or disabled. Naturally, we need to implement a planning solution that will address all these concerns. You don't need to worry anymore. The best part is that you don't need any special skill or expertise to manage this plan. You don't need to take a hundred seminars and webinars to become an expert at executing this plan. Which is good as I speak for myself, but if I take a hundred seminars on a good majority of subjects, I may not necessarily become better at them. I will just have taken a hundred seminars. You will have automatic confidence and success.

Here is the kicker. This is not some newfangled, fancy financial technique only the rich and famous can implement. Almost anyone can employ this tool. This tool is a *life insurance policy*! I know there are some of you that are now screaming the word *what* at the top of your lungs. Some of you are probably asking, "You mean this (fill in your special adjective here) guy is trying to get me to buy a life insurance policy?" Some of you are spilling your morning coffee and cereal all over the house. I will not be coming over to clean it up, I assure you. As you read on, you will see that this amazing product or tool, as I like to call it, however, will be able to alleviate all the concerns we have mentioned before. In some ways, I understand that there are some negative feelings about the product, and, in some ways, it has not garnered the best reputation it probably should have. And we will explore that now.

Why All This Perceived Negativity?

The biggest reason, I believe, for the perceived negativity is the fact that talking about this means that we must face the prospect of our own mortality. Unfortunately, besides our name, parents, and birthday, the other thing each one of us will surely have is a date of death. I hate to be the bearer of bad news, but ignoring it will not stop its reality or potentially disastrous consequences you could have by not planning for it, at least financially. The other reason for its bad rep is that you may have to keep it for a potentially long time and pay into it for that length of time to see its benefit of money paid to someone else upon death. To me this is good. This means you are alive and kicking. I know it takes discipline to keep it up, but you need discipline in everything if you want to succeed. Some people regard owning life insurance as a luxury, almost like house painting. It is a nice luxury to have, but with everything else going on, it will wait until later.

There is one other historical factor for this negativity. I will very briefly go over it. In the 1980s, we saw a big boon with interest rate earnings on investments. You could even earn as much as 12% on a bank CD. Life insurance policies were sold through illustrations. These were merely projections on how your policy was supposed to perform throughout its lifetime. Agents and their associated companies were showing illustrations with high interest rates, and these rates were supposed to continue for the rest of the policy and the insured's life. Theoretically, because the interest rates were high, there would be an opportunity for the premiums to vanish. That meant that there would be a time that a client would be able to stop paying premiums forever, and the policy would be able to sustain itself forever through its cash value growth. One problem. The 1990s happened. Interest rates had bottomed out, and ten years or so later from that time in the middle of the 1980s, when policies grossly underperformed and the premiums that were promised to vanish never did, many class action suits (especially against the largest life insurance companies) were filed. Clients eventually won those suits. The fact that clients won, though, in my opinion, does not matter. The fact that these suits were filed in the first place was enough to give the insurance industry a black eye. To this day, we are still slowly but surely recovering our once positive image.

As an aside, I will opine again. In the eighties, there was a common financial mantra that "you should buy term and invest the difference." This was because just about every other product in the financial world would, or potentially could, offer a higher investment rate of return than permanent life insurance policies. Why? Those products had no mortality charge that life insurance policies had. I feel that companies and their agents stressed too much on investment benefits and very little on the insurance benefits. In other words, they were not true to themselves. They wanted to try to compete with securities houses and banks for investment dollars. This was not and still is not a race that insurance companies are supposed to compete in. It is like heavyweight weightlifters competing against world-class swimmers in swimming races, if you can imagine what that image would look like. If these companies had just held the fort, stayed true to themselves, and emphasized the insurance benefits to clients and prospective clients, they could've saved themselves a lot of perpetual aggravation. That is my two cents' worth anyway.

How Does This Tool Work?

You might have heard some of the names used. You might have heard of "ten-year level term life," "second to die life," and "whole life with the term rider." You might feel overwhelmed and a sense of "Why should I bother with this?" Let's make it easier for you. There are two basic types of life insurance policies: term insurance and permanent insurance.

Term insurance is easiest to explain. Essentially, you pay a fixed annual or a more frequent period premium for a certain amount of insurance or death benefit. The initial premiums are less expensive, but after a certain term or years, your premium will increase. You are essentially initially paying lower premiums for a higher death benefit, but there are no other living benefits other than the security of knowing that you are taking care of your family financially upon your death. It is analogous to renting a home. You pay a monthly rent to a landlord, but other than living space, you receive no other benefit.

The permanent insurance, on the other hand, works differently. The permanent policies' premiums are much more expensive initially but level throughout the insured's lifetime. These are the plans that build up cash value, which gives you equity in your policy. These are the plans that you can cash out, surrender for its cash value, or even borrow against. I, however, like to use the term *cash value you can access in some fashion*, and I will discuss this later as we travel through the book. The type of policy that I am going to emphasize for the most part is the permanent type. I believe that this is type of life insurance policy that can fix the mistakes we have mentioned previously. However, the fact is that all types of policies offer the most important part of any life insurance policy, and that, of course, is the death benefit. When I meet with clients and they tell me that the permanent policies are not affordable or even desired, but they want the term insurance because of the lower cost and higher death benefit, then term is what they shall have. Keep in mind that term insurance allows the client to change to a permanent plan through its conversion privilege. If the insurance to be changed is going to be the same or less than the original term policy's amount of insurance, then no evidence of insurability is needed. In layman's terms, that means you can keep your blood, and we won't snoop around for records from your physician. And you will have this guaranteed death benefit on the permanent policy automatically approved.

There is one more type of policy that we use quite often in our planning practice because of its versatility. This type of policy can act like a term insurance or act like a permanent insurance policy. I would call this sort of like a hybrid type of policy. This type of policy is called a universal life policy. To understand how this policy works, think of a chameleon and how the reptile changes its color to blend in its environment. Just like any other insurance policy, there is a minimum premium payment that must be paid to keep the insurance in force or active. The beautiful main feature of this type of policy is its flexible premium design. You can add additional premium anytime. You can make it a recurring monthly addition or as a large lump sum. Everything is up to you. The only limit is by what the contract allows. When you pay the minimum premium on this policy, the policy acts like a term insurance policy. It will give a client a death benefit that will be guaranteed at a certain period, but it will not necessarily build any cash value or equity. Oftentimes, I like to use this type of policy for seniors as a term insurance alternative. This is because most senior citizens would not qualify for most term insurance because of age. If you add premium at any point, then this policy acts like a permanent insurance policy that will build cash value as well as give a guaranteed death benefit.

Essentially, what happens here is the insurance company uses this extra premium to build up your cash value for you. That is why I like to use the analogy of the chameleon. The policy is going to change its character based on the environment you are choosing to create. Would you want more death benefit or more death benefit and cash value?

Within the universal life insurance policy family, there is one policy that is being offered a lot today. I have mixed opinions on this type of policy, but I will explain how it works. This policy is called an equity index universal life insurance policy. The idea of this policy is that the cash value is based upon investment results on certain equity indices—for example, the Standard & Poor's index or the Nasdaq index. The idea is if these indices rise, your cash value will rise also. If those indices lose money, the interest credited on these policies stays the same as the previous year. You do not lose cash value. Why I have a mixed view on policies like this is because, again, there is no guaranteed cash value here, and guaranteed interest rate is, for the most part, lower than what a permanent whole life type of policy would offer. So to achieve the maximum cash value benefits of the policy, the crediting indices must also be earning high interest. Many of my colleagues will aggressively offer these types of policies to their clients because they want to allow the client to have the feeling that there is an investment component to it where very high returns can be attained. Having said that, I believe these policies are also very good policies, and they have their uses also. And we still use them for our clients also. I will urge you, however, if you are offered this type of policy to purchase, make sure that you do your common sense due diligence. Believe it or not, you now know more about life insurance than about 95% of the population. This isn't so bad, is it?

Great! I'll Be Worth More Dead than Alive!

This is another statement that I've heard more times than I can count. On the surface, this appears to be a morbid statement. And it is not a pleasant statement to hear. I believe it is said in jest most of the time, but it stems from the fact that a client may feel that he or she has an extremely large amount of insurance and to procure more would not make any financial or possibly emotional sense. What people do not take into consideration, however, is the time value of money factor. For example, in 1964, when my parents married each other, they bought a three-bedroom, 3,000-square-foot Colonial-style home in a middle to upper-middle-class neighborhood in Brooklyn, NY. They bought this home for $27,000. Would anybody or everybody love to buy that type of home for that price now! Their mortgage payment at that time was $294 per month for thirty years. For this price today, you could have a new compact car or a very good late-model used car if you are lucky. My parents each had good jobs working for New York City to be able to scrape up enough money every month to pay that while today, for most people, $294 a month may not be a big financial stretch. Why is that? This is because of our friend inflation. Inflation eats at the value of money. Please remember the rule of seventy-two, which states that the number seventy-two divided by the interest rate in question is the length of years that it would take for the purchasing power or value of this money to either halve or double depending on the direction of the value you want to calculate. For example, at an 8% interest rate, the purchasing power of your money will be half or double its present value in nine years.

Let's say you are a thirty-five-year-old, and you have one million dollars of life insurance. A large amount, you say? We'll see. Assume a 4% inflation rate (which is generally what it is around most of the time). If your death occurred at age fifty-three or eighteen years later, that $1 million would have the purchasing power of $500,000 today. Not terrible. But live another eighteen years and have your death be at age seventy-one, now that $1 million would be worth $250,000. This is a 75% erosion of purchasing power. So even if you have a large amount of insurance, you will need to factor in the time value of money concept because inflation always exists.

Life Insurance Is a Bad Investment

This statement is another gem. I answer this by saying that life insurance is not really an investment. If you want to think of an investment as a vehicle that if you put in $1.00 now and you will have $1.10 next month, then this is not the type of product that this is. In fact, life insurance is just that—insurance. If I submit new paperwork to an insurance company on behalf of a client that says, "The purpose of this insurance is for investment-related purposes." That is profanity or heresy to an insurance company. They become extremely annoyed. They send the paperwork back to me to amend this explanation. Insurance companies by nature are extremely conservative. They want to be fully transparent to the consumer. I would imagine that is what you would want an insurance company to be. After all, who else is going to pay a family a potentially large sum of money when it would be most needed in exchange for a small and manageable premium to be paid over time? In fact, all things being equal in terms of the purposes for investment, generally I would say the vast majority of financial vehicles are better because they can offer higher interest rates, and they do not factor in a mortality charge that a life insurance company must charge in their policies in order for this product to be considered an insurance policy. The reason that people should employ this tool in their financial planning is because there is some need for life insurance.

I Don't Trust Insurance Agents. They Only Want to Make a Large Commission at My Expense.

In a way, I do appreciate the honesty that some people have when they make a statement like that. I would be lying if I said that everyone in my profession were saints, and unfortunately, that is not always the case. Understand something, though: every profession has their excellent people who care about their clients, and they have their people who are dishonest to the point of criminality. The financial service profession is no different. Some of you might have received this book from your insurance agent or financial planner. My guess is he or she gave the book to you to introduce you to this new way of how to spend or invest your money wisely so that you will be financially secure.

As for us earning commission, well, this is how we are compensated. If you are working with an independent agent, such as myself, keep in mind each company will compensate us separately. This gives us the freedom to be as objective as we can and be flexible when we structure plans for clients. There are still agents in our profession called captive agents. These are agents who can only represent one company and no one else. This is not as common today as it was in the past. These agents are considered pseudo-employees by the companies they represent. This means they have company-sponsored health insurance and/or retirement plans, which contribute to insurance company costs. In this era of companies looking to cut costs, the captive agent route is not as common. Still, he or she will be able to objectively structure the correct plan for you based on what his or her company offers, but just know it is only for one company. When a family suffers because of a loved one's death, I can tell you the first call survivors and potential beneficiaries make is to a life insurance agent. These people know that while everyone else asks for money, the life insurance agent is the only person who has the potential to effectuate someone giving money.

When I myself receive this type of call, I say one of two statements: either "You can relax. Your relative had purchased a policy through me, and I can help you get started processing the required paperwork so that you can receive the money that the policy promised" or "I am sorry, but your relative did not take advantage of our offer for insurance. I wish I could be more helpful. Sorry again. Please extend my condolences to the family." From an emotional standpoint, none of these calls is desirable, but as a professional, I would rather be able to tell the caller the former statement. But, again, I will caution everybody to do your due diligence to the person that you are going to work with. Ask about his credentials. All life insurance agents are licensed in the states where they do business, so you can ask for his license number, and he or she will gladly give it to you, and you can investigate any complaints that might be against this agent. Please know that most agents, just like most professionals in most professions, are looking out for their clients' best interests.

A few final points before I leave this section. A big reason that sometimes there is an unsuccessful adviser-client relationship is that upon meeting the adviser for the first time, the client fails to be specific about what they are looking for. To illustrate this, allow me to use these two examples. When you are ill, you would not say to a doctor, "Hello, Doctor. I am not feeling well. Can you just please write me a prescription so I can feel better?" When you dine out at your favorite restaurant and the server asks for your order, you generally would not say, "I don't know. Please stick some food on my plate, and then you can bring me my check." These examples sound funny, ridiculous, and extreme, but the point is, clients have at times when meeting me for the first time will say to me, "I would like to have a good college funding plan" or "How much is the cost or premium for this insurance?" These statements offer me nothing that I can use to formulate the best plan for the client because there is no specificity as to their goals, needs, and wants. Better to say to an adviser, "I would like a plan that will insure me for $400,000 and also generate $150,000 in cash value in twenty years if at all possible" or "I would very much like to have a plan that will allow me to withdraw $60,000 per year for the rest of my life in thirty years when I reach sixty-five years old." Now I have something to work with. Having said all of that, not only should you be specific, but you also need to be a little flexible. The request you state may not be fulfilled for whatever reason, but there could be, out of necessity, a small alteration that needs to be done. Therefore, you need to keep a good line of communication open. You need to be frank with your adviser about material things he needs to know about. For example, your financial goals, your current status, your health status, and your perceived barriers to plan execution, etc.

Advisers, I am not letting you off the hook on this one. This includes myself also, so now I am going to yell at myself also. We must do a lot better in what I call the QASU method of communication. This stands for "question and shut up." We must be better at asking questions and listening. If you will be less dogmatic and judgmental and be more flexible in your plan designs, if you will listen more, ask more questions, and talk less, clients will be more apt to being more open about giving their information to you.

Getting back to you, my friends and prospective clients. If you are not prepared and open with your adviser, what tends to happen is that an adviser will have to show you more options than is necessary. This leads to analysis paralysis on your part and frustration on the adviser's part, so what generally happens is that you will take the path of least resistance and do nothing. If you do that, no one benefits because you still do not possess what you were looking for. This could have been avoided with proper communication from the outset. To summarize, a successful adviser (agent)-client relationship can only be built with trust, respect, and frank communication from both sides. If this is achieved, I promise you now that you will be richly rewarded with lifetime financial security because it will be much easier to start and continue your one-step financial success plan.

College Funding: The Solution

Here's What You've Been Waiting For

Now let's apply this tool to help us through our cycle of life milestones. We will start with college funding. I first want to clarify something. I will be using the words *tool* and *product* interchangeably. You have probably noticed this already. I will say that the best time to employ life insurance as a college funding vehicle is at the birth of your child, if not earlier than his birth. Of course, if you didn't do that, don't worry; it will still work well. A policy can be structured one of three ways. The first way is to buy a certain amount of insurance. You will pay whatever that premium is to keep the insurance in force. This will generate a certain amount of cash value. This cash value is based directly on the amount of insurance or death benefit of the policy.

The second way is basically the opposite way. You will pay a certain premium, and that will purchase a certain amount of insurance. The insurance or death benefit is what your cash surrender value is based on, as you now know. All things being equal, the higher the insurance amount, the larger the cash value that you will obtain. Or the third way is for the agent to customize a policy that will produce a certain cash value at a certain time period. Usually, you would want this desired cash value at the year of the policy that corresponds to the year that your child turns eighteen or at the year of your child's college entrance as a freshman. If you do, however, structure your policy this way, more than likely this would require the most premium to be paid out of your pocket, but in return, this will guarantee that you will have the cash value that you want at the time that you want it.

Two beautiful benefits of life insurance are the cash value you can use for college education and that cash can be taken systematically through its loan provision. I will explain more how the loan provision works in the next section. Then this money is tax-free. Think of it—for every $100 earned as life insurance cash value, that would equate to earning approximately $130 in any other investment, with this $30 difference going toward tax payments on the gains made from other investment vehicles. There is one exception to the concept that cash value in a life insurance policy is tax-free. If you cash surrender the policy for its full cash value, the amount of cash value over the amount you've paid in premiums will be treated as taxable income to you. Also, as I mentioned before, what people do not realize is that the cash value in a life insurance policy will not be used by the government, colleges, or universities in calculating how much financial aid your child will receive. Needs-based financial aid is based on what they (the government or educational institutions) expect you to contribute as far as tuition payments. And this is determined by your assets and your income amounts you disclose on the FAFSA. The FAFSA is an abbreviation for Free Application for Federal Student Aid. This is the form that must be completed to receive any kind of needs-based aid. As of now, life insurance cash value and annuity account balances are excluded in calculating what a family's expected contribution should be. Which, of course, for you this is wonderful because if they also knew that you had substantial cash value in life insurance policies, that could adversely affect whether your child would receive financial assistance. As an extreme example, let's say that both parents were destitute. I mean to the point where their bed was basically a bunch of pizza boxes covered with diapers, and they had little income. The only money they did have was $500,000 in cash value from old life insurance policies. These parents could get away with telling the US government and prospective educational institutions that we have very little income, and we have very little assets, and that is what the government and schools would have to abide by.

Here is another cherry to put on this low-fat, delicious-tasting financial cake. Some firms like mine will work with a scholarship service. They will offer reward points that can be converted into tuition dollars for certain schools. The only responsibility on your part is to procure and maintain a permanent life insurance policy. These scholarships can sometimes total to one year of free tuition at these participating schools. This could be on top of any other scholarship offered or amount you have accumulated. This has nothing to do with academics or need. It is offered simply because you are doing what you are supposed to be doing anyway, which is to systematically save for college education expenses for your children.

How on Earth can you beat that! Even if you have waited to start saving for education funding, you still could legally reposition assets into life insurance policies or annuities to have their values not count toward financial aid. Try all this with mutual funds or other investments. Remember, I spoke about insuring your college funding program in case of death. Well, here is your solution. Procure enough insurance to make sure that amount is paid to the family in the event of death. Simple enough? For example, if you expect tuition or other expenses to total $250,000 over four years you must insure yourself for $250,000 at least. The good news is that the more insurance you carry, the greater the cash value potentially. This, of course, is assuming you purchased permanent coverage.

Retirement Funding: The Solution

Let's Keep it Going!

How do we properly apply life insurance planning to retirement planning? If you remember from our previous section on retirement planning, the dilemmas you will recall there are two main concerns. One concern that is addressed by almost every advisor is, of course, the accumulation of funds for retirement, and the other problem is how your family will pay the taxes on their inherited tax-qualified plan assets. This, if also you recall from the last section, is a very overlooked problem that I am addressing in this book. As I mentioned, the permanent life insurance policy will be the solution here. Let's examine how the insurance can be used to fund retirement.

Quite honestly, for the most part, the life insurance methods you can use to fund retirement planning are the same as you would use to fund college education. Let's review. They were to procure a certain amount of insurance and pay its corresponding premium. Pay a certain premium, and receive the appropriate amount of insurance that premium buys, or you could set a cash value goal for a certain time, say age sixty-five, and customize a mix of premium and insurance option that provides the desired financial amount at that age. The main difference between using a permanent life insurance policy for retirement planning versus college funding is that when you use a life insurance for retirement planning, you can expect to take funds or distributions out of the policy over a longer period systematically through its loan provision feature. "How do the loan provisions work in a life insurance policy?" you may ask. I will address this now. First, I want you to think of driving your car. You do not have to fill your car with gas each time you want to drive. You don't even have to fill your gas tank to the point that it is always full. At some point, though, you will have to fill your car tank with gas. Either that or you better be as strong as an ox so that you can push the car everywhere. Please remember this analogy as you keep reading.

With permanent policies, remember, these are your whole life policies or your universal life policies that you are paying more than the minimum premium so that it generates cash value. As you pay premiums into the policy, one part goes toward the costs for maintaining the insurance and other expenses. And the rest is invested into cash value.

I will introduce you to the term *basis*. *Basis* simply means the amount you've paid into the policy via premiums in its simplest terms. If an amount you access from the cash value from a life insurance policy is equal to or lower than your basis (the premiums you have paid), it is not considered it a loan at all. It is basically a return of premium. For example, if you access $100,000 of cash value but you've paid $100,000 in premiums into the policy previously, none of the $100,000 is subject to loans. There is a big misconception here. Most people believe that you must start paying loans from the first dollar you access. The good news is that this is untrue. I know what some of you are thinking. *I want no part of loans. I have a car loan, mortgage, etc. I do not want to have to deal with another type of loan payment every month. Thank you.* This will be different, I promise.

A loan payment starts on any cash value amount after the basis. At that point, the insurance company moves the loan amount from your cash value into a separate account. This is after the insurance company gives you a check for the amount you requested. Now, this separate account charges interest just like any other loan, so let's say 4% interest. Remember, though, your regular cash value account is still earning interest on the remaining cash value still there. Again, let's also say about 4% interest. What this means is that your net interest charge to you is 0%. How about that! Try obtaining a 0% interest loan from a bank with an option to pay it back at some point in the future instead of the next month and hope they don't throw you out of the premises while laughing at you.

Now, what happens if you don't physically pay it back? It is paid back with the proceeds upon death. Here is another beautiful benefit with cash value policies, especially your whole life insurance. They have PUAs, which is short for paid-up additions, which raise the insurance amount over time. These are added to your insurance amount upon death to maintain the tax-favored status of life insurance. One of the benefits of favored tax status of life insurance is that the proceeds are paid to a beneficiary (or beneficiaries) tax-free. What this means is that for the policy to be considered a life insurance policy, there should be a mathematical relationship between the cash value and death benefit that must always be attained. How this relationship is determined is beyond the scope of this book. But all you need to know is that the addition of PUAs is a blessing for you. This loan is against the cash value, not from the cash value.

Let's look at an example to illustrate. You had a large $500,000 death benefit policy for fifteen years. You had paid premiums totaling $100,000. You have $250,000 of cash value. You wish to borrow $200,000 from the policy. With the PUAs, your death benefit now is $625,000. Here's how this transaction would look. The first $100,000 accessed is not an amount that is borrowed. There are no loans to be paid back. This is your basis. Only the excess $100,000 that you borrowed is subject to loan repayment. The insurance company sends you a check for $200,000. Then they move the excess $100,000 from your cash value and put it into a separate loan account. This account charges you an interest rate, say 4%. You still are earning interest of 4% on your existing cash value, just as you had been normally doing on your regular cash value account before requesting the money. If your death occurs the same day you receive your $200,000 check, the beneficiaries would receive it. This $200,000 is received tax-free.

$625,000 (the beginning death benefit + PUAs) - $100,000 (loan amount) = $525,000 (to beneficiary or beneficiaries)

Amazing! Even with the loan, your beneficiaries will receive more insurance than when you purchased the policy, and you will receive a nice check from the cash value you've earned. As for tax treatment of this money, as you know, life insurance proceeds are not subject to income tax by beneficiaries. As for receipt of cash value, let me ask you, "If you have a car loan or mortgage loan or both, do you pay tax on the money you receive?" The answer is of course not. You pay taxes to acquire or sell the asset but not on the loan payment. How does this come together for saving for retirement? The plan is to start a permanent policy as early as you can, and then make systematic withdrawals over time. This is where your pension comes in.

If you remember very early on in the book, I spoke about having a pension and why corporations do not offer pensions. But that doesn't mean that you can't have the pension on your own. Essentially, this means that you can create your own pension this way by building enough funds that over time, at some point in the future, you can take systematic withdrawals from every year, and there's your pension.

One word of caution about loans. If you remember the analogy of filling the car with gas, you know if you do not fill the car at some point, you will not have enough gas to keep moving or start the car. Life insurance policy loans work the same way. If you do not have enough cash value to support the systematic withdrawals, then there is a danger of the policy lapsing. Please make sure that you work with your adviser to guarantee that you will always be in a good position with your policy.

Death, Taxes, and Qualified Plans Revisited

I am going to revisit an issue that I have spent a good deal of time speaking about in the earliest section about retirement planning dilemmas. Again, this is an extremely overlooked issue, even by most advisers, because when it hits you, there is nothing that can be done at that point if it had not been personally planned for, and that is the tax treatment of qualified plans upon death. Hopefully, you remember and have internalized the mantra that a tax-qualified plan is the worst place to have money upon your death. I will review if you have not. If this money is left to a spouse, then it is tax-deferred because of the spousal deduction. Again, this is only a deferral of tax, not an avoidance of taxes. This only gives the money in the plan the time needed to grow bigger because of interest earnings and contributions from the spouse that is still alive, if any. When the second spouse dies, the next beneficiaries are going to receive a very large tax bill. When a nonspouse is a beneficiary, he or she receives the plan's assets upon the plan holder's death. This beneficiary will pay income taxes on this money based on his tax bracket with the addition of this money. Based on 2019 brackets, it might not be that difficult to reach 37%, which is the highest tax bracket now (or whatever it will be at that time). That means it could very well be higher. Remember from earlier the examples of my mother and the married couple Tom and Dana. My mother's children—of course, I am one, but you knew that—and the couple's children had to pay $115,000 and the taxes that resulted from the $976,000 respectively. These are large amounts. So what is the solution? My mother, Tom, and Dana needed to procure enough life insurance so that the children would be able pay these taxes. The beneficiaries would have used the life insurance proceeds to pay the taxes, and no one would have to physically come up with money out of their pockets to pay these taxes. In short, you keep your money, and "someone else's" money pays these taxes.

There are two tips I will recommend before closing. Please work with your agent or adviser over time in order to take snapshots of your qualified retirement plan growth and your balances, and have your adviser make projections of what plans can accumulate over time. You should do this to make sure the life insurance portfolio you possess is current and can be as accurate as possible. More than likely, you will never be 100% accurate because of all the variables involved, but in any case, your heirs should never be in a position to lose half or more of their money to pay income taxes on your death. Remember, your goal is to keep as much money as you can. I don't have to tell you that the goal of the government is to take as much of this money as it can from you.

The second tip is that a special type of life insurance policy would work very well here if you are a couple. It's called a survivorship universal life policy. Essentially, it is a universal life policy that covers two lives together. It is one policy that pays the death benefit on the second insured's death. There are many reasons why this is a wonderful alternative. First, you can make your nonspouse retirement plan the main beneficiary of the policy. This means, for example, that as we have learned, if your children are to receive qualified plan benefit assets, then they will be the ones to pay the tax on these benefits. With a survivorship universal life insurance policy, the same children will be the beneficiaries of the insurance policies. And they ostensibly will use these proceeds to pay the resulting taxes.

Another big advantage is that the premiums paid into these types of policies are lower than if you had two separate policies. This is because the insurance company is evaluating and assessing the health risk of two lives together, and this also leads to the third advantage. Since the insurance company is evaluating the risk or underwriting the policy based on two lives together, if one partner's health is impaired to the point where procuring their own policy is either too costly or the insurance is impossible to obtain, they can still be insured on the survivorship policy as long as their partner's health is reasonably good. Please remember with the survivorship policy, though, when the first insured dies, the second insured still must maintain premium payments. Also, the partners cannot make each other first beneficiaries on the policy.

If you don't mind these minor disadvantages, a survivorship universal life policy is a wonderful alternative for a couple when appropriate. Just as a quick aside before I leave this time, traditionally, advisers were using these policies in conjunction with certain trusts to protect potential inherited assets and to provide the funds to pay the resulting estate taxes (or the inheritance tax). I spoke about the taxes in a previous section, so I will not go over it here, and I will ask you to refer to the earlier section. Since those funding thresholds have become very high, and these taxes will not apply to most people, most of the advisers basically consider the survivorship policies dead or useless and won't even offer them. Useless like cassettes and typewriters. Do they even make these anymore? I use survivorship policies all the time in my practice, obviously. Unlike Frankenstein's monster, this is a good thing to bring back to life, and it won't physically destroy too many cities. If you feel your situation may warrant it, you should bring it up to your adviser or agent to determine if indeed it is a good fit.

Living Retired: The Solution

Most of the time when I speak about the group I am calling "living retired," the members of this group are generally your senior citizens. Most of the people in this group may also have the same needs as anyone else. They have grandchildren they are helping to fund education. They have qualified retirement plans with large accumulated balances. Admittedly, one of my biggest challenges is advising them that yes, life insurance can be a vital solution to their pressing financial concerns. Sometimes the biggest challenge for them is to find the premium to fund the policy. I will show you how that is possible to do, and you might not even have to pay for it out of your pocket. I do submit to you that most of the need for life insurance at this stage of life are not for wealth accumulation, but it is generally for wealth protection and legacy planning. Anyway, let's move forward.

Reverse Mortgages Revisited

If you remember, we spoke about this financial tool before, but to review, these loans essentially convert home equity to physical cash with a mortgage company or bank serving as the middleman. These middlemen give you the cash and in return, place a financial lien on the home to be paid back at some point. As we've learned, this lien is paid back by the heirs when the last named mortgagor dies. For example, a husband and wife takes out the reverse mortgage together. The wife is the second person to die, and the children inherit the home. They will inherit the home, but they will also inherit the accompanying debt to be paid back to the bank. This is where the life insurance solution comes to the rescue. Very simply, this couple or this single person who took the reverse mortgage will procure enough life insurance coverage to pay the heirs (children) the money they need to pay back the bank.

The life insurance will pay the beneficiary within a month or two, and the heirs can write a check to the bank for the amount of the loan, and now they will have a home free and clear of debt. They could do whatever they want with the home. Ideally, the reverse mortgage borrowers should take out the life insurance for the highest amount the loan balance can reach, but financially or otherwise, that might not be possible. Even if they covered a part of the loan, this would be helpful to the heirs because even if they had to sell the home quickly to pay the debt, the insurance proceeds could replace the equity that they could lose on sale of a home.

For example, these reverse mortgage clients have a home that is worth $900,000, but the home has a $400,000 reverse mortgage loan on it when the heirs inherit the home. Ideally, this home should sell for $900,000 on fair market value. But this home had been quickly sold for $600,000. The parents did procure $300,000 of life insurance to cover part of the loan several years earlier. The heirs received $600,000 from the home sale plus $300,000 from the life insurance, paid back the $400,000 loan, and netted $500,000 for themselves. Obviously, not an ideal situation because they do not have the physical property anymore, but they made the best out of this bad situation. Keep in mind that if the parents had not purchased this $300,000 life insurance policy, the heirs would probably not have anything. They would have had to sell more quickly than they did and run the risk of selling it at an even lower value than they did or risk having the bank take the home and sell it through the foreclosure process.

Remember, also in this case of the heirs inheriting a home with a reverse mortgage lien placed on it, the bank has to potentially wait a long time for repayment of the loan, so when they realize that they can receive their payoff any day, they are like sharks smelling bloody prey. They will call the heirs daily about making the payment like collection agents. I've received many calls from the beneficiaries of my clients' life insurance policies, and they have shared their horror stories about intensive, almost abusive bank harassment. This was done generally over the phone, but in some instances, the bank would write. Of course, the banks do not remind these people that they have one year from the date of the last mortgagor's death to satisfy the loan, but the banks do not care. If they can harass people for repayment, they will. Banks know the heirs can basically giveaway the home to them, and the misery of a large loan balance will hang over the heirs' heads no more

What is interesting in this case with the above example is it's almost like the heirs sold the parent's home, which had become their home when the parents died, for the fair market value, and they satisfied the outstanding mortgage on their terms or on the day they wanted to and not what when some lender forces them to. One final tip: like I mentioned before, the survivorship universal life insurance policy is an outstanding product to purchase if you are a couple. In fact, to cover a reverse mortgage loan amount may be the best use of this type of policy. Since the heirs are the ones that will have to pay the debt, they will be the beneficiaries of this policy.

My Heirs Are Adults. I've Worked Hard for My Money. They Should Be Able to Handle This on Their Own. I Don't See Where This Life Insurance Will Help Me.

First of all, I will not make judgments on this statement. I know that this is essentially a personal value judgment, and if that is your feeling about the subject of life insurance, then I will treat this with the utmost respect. I also know that there might be valid reasons on your part for feeling this way. I will say that the premise of my book is to implement some legacy planning. This is what life insurance is about. Bluntly but respectfully, I will say this. If legacy planning does not occupy some priority in your financial planning life, then life insurance will probably be of no help to you. I do hate to say this, though, that maybe this is not a book to read or use for you. This is not just for seniors but for all who are reading and hopefully enjoying and learning from the book. For those living in retirement, you also should keep in mind that your children or your heirs have careers and families of their own, and this provides them their own life opportunities and problems. So, to worry about the financial problems of Mom and Dad also just complicates their lives, and I don't believe that this is really a legacy you would want to leave for them. If, however, this statement is made because of financial apprehension, then I say to you, "Don't worry," although here it is more important than ever to meet with a competent adviser or agent so that a solution that you can feel satisfied with and happy about can be obtained.

What about Medicaid Planning?

As discussed earlier, wealth preservation is a big problem, especially in the senior citizen population. Our life expectancies are now until our late seventies and early eighties. Almost 70% of people over the age of sixty-five will require chronic care or long-term care later in life for an average of three years, and 20% of those people will need it for longer than five years.

This, my friends, is what I would call a serious concern. Unfortunately, the care has to be paid for. It would be better for you to pay for it than the government through the Medicaid program. If Medicaid steps in, it is because you have depleted all of your assets except for a small amount of cash and a very small "burial" life insurance policy. I suggest that your planning start as soon as possible. You need to use the traditional methods of transferring assets into certain trusts or even to other people quickly because of the lookback periods that will start at an unknown point in time. Purchasing long-term care insurance is always a good bet to provide funds for home or nursing care. The only issue with long-term care insurance, however, is that many companies have pulled out of the market, and there are very strict underwriting or evaluation requirements.

The good news is that life insurance can be a viable alternative or a compliment to the traditional methods of Medicaid planning. Firstly, of course, you can use your cash surrender value. Secondly, there is a better option, and this is where many life insurers have gotten smarter and more progressive. They have added something called accelerated benefit riders. What this basically means is that under certain circumstances, you could take an advance of your death benefit money. Usually, this is for situations where you need money to pay for chronic or long-term care or for a critical illness. A critical illness is defined as cancer, stroke, heart attack, etc. Any money not used will be left as a traditional life insurance benefit to be paid to the beneficiaries upon death. There is no extra premium for this because, essentially, all the life insurance companies are doing is turning the death benefit into a pool of money that can be accessed while the insured is alive under certain circumstances. In my opinion, I think they're doing this because of the dearth of viable long-term care insurance policy options.

It's My Policy, and I'll Sell It if I Want To

Another beautiful way life insurance can help with this type of wealth preservation planning is for you, the policyholder, to simply sell the interest in your life insurance policy on the open market. Most people do not realize that life insurance is an asset that can be sold just like your home or your car. What happens here is that an investor or a company will buy your policy for some percent of your death benefit and then get the full death benefit upon your death. This investor also maintains the premium payments needed to make sure the policy stays in force for the life of the insured. This is called a life settlement. You might have heard of the term *viatical settlements*. The concept is essentially the same. The only major difference is a viatical settlement is a sale of a policy of a terminally-ill insured. The life settlement is the sale of a policy from a higher-age senior or a policy from someone younger with a severe health impairment.

How much a policyholder can receive from a sale, though, depends on many factors. What investors want to determine is your projected life expectancy. All things being equal, the policies that can be sold for the largest percent of death benefit are the ones from those policyholders who have severely impaired health or are healthy higher-age seniors. In essence, the shorter the insured's life expectancy, the higher the amount that can be received on a sale. The long and short of this is that a sale of your life insurance policy can net you thousands of dollars for you to do whatever you want. Since the investor is now paying the required premiums, you as an insured will receive the corresponding premium relief. This also can be worth thousands of dollars. It is as if you refinanced your home for a lower rate without giving years of paid mortgage to a bank in return. You probably at this point will never need to try to qualify for Medicaid because you will now have the funds you need for long-term care expenses. You will probably receive better care in my opinion because as the saying goes "money talks."

A couple of tips, though, make sure that you really do not want or can't afford this policy. Obviously, you won't have it anymore. Also make sure that the policy has an assignability clause. This is what allows the policyholder to sell his policy. The sale is technically a permanent assignment to a new policy owner. Most companies offer this on their policies, but some companies do not. If you are not sure, then ask your adviser. Make sure you will be working with a company that does offer it if you are contemplating a life settlement transaction at some time in the future. I can tell you that my firm has been able to provide thousands of dollars to clients by helping them execute these life settlement transactions.

RMDs Are A-OK

"Okay, Mr. Hotshot Insurance Guy, you. Now that you are telling me that I can and should purchase life insurance at my age, it would be nice if you also told me how to pay for this wonderful insurance." To this, I'll say, "Oofah! I love a challenge!" First of all, I will reiterate what I said before. Just like anything else you want to purchase in life, if you see it as something of value, you will somehow figure out a way to obtain the funds to purchase it. Hopefully, I have added value in your mind about the value and wonders of insurance. If not, then you probably will not take the actions required to purchase insurance. Here is something that should help. There is a way to find the funds for the life insurance. If you are age seventy and a half or older, you will know what I am referring to.

If you have a qualified retirement plan, please note that on April 1 of the year after you turn seventy and a half years old, you will be forced to withdraw money from your qualified retirement plan. This is the government's way of "punishing you" because you have the audacity to want to keep money in your own plan and want to withdraw it on your terms. They will want you to start taking withdrawals not because they want you to have a little extra spending cash to enjoy or for you to be a little more financially comfortable. They want you to withdraw these funds because by doing so, the government can start taxing you on it. Isn't that what your primary goal in your retired life should be? To give the government some of your hard-earned accumulated retirement money? Failure or refusal to take this distribution will subject the plan holder to a 50% penalty on the required amount that had to be withdrawn. For example, let's suppose the government sends you a statement telling you that you need to take a required minimum distribution of $5,000. You fail to take this distribution. Not only are you subject to the resulting tax, but on top of that, you are also subject to an extra $2,500 penalty. Not bad, huh? No, actually, that does sound bad and unfair, but the government would like very much to have some of your money, and this way is as good as any. And by the way, don't worry. The government will tell you every year how much you need to withdraw.

For most seniors, this is not money that they would normally use. They just find it as annoying to have. So, what can you do with it? How about using it for a life insurance premium? Now at least you have a use for this money that you would not have had otherwise, and upon your death, you will leave a legacy of much more money than would have ever accumulated in your retirement plan.

The Gift That Keeps on Giving

This section is not going to necessarily deal with financial needs, but it is certainly something that we would all like to accomplish. The vast majority of us would like to leave a legacy to someone other than family. In other words, make a positive contribution to the world. Most people want to give his or her money to causes or organizations that they believe in. I believe that this is something we should all be doing. We should not only be doing this because of the benefits to other people. We should also be giving for our own spiritual and psychological well-being. Obviously, here we will deal with giving financially.

Let me ask you. Ever wondered how one little fruit on one fruit-bearing tree can eventually multiply to be many pieces of fruit for many fruit trees all over the world? It is very simple. An animal eats the fruit, and the fruit has seeds. These animals biologically excrete the seeds somewhere else, and eventually, they grow to be other fruit trees. If a bird eats the fruit, he can fly anywhere else far from where the original tree was planted, and eventually, a tree will grow there. By implementing life insurance planning into your philanthropic giving program, you can actually give a small amount of money, which is your premium (or seeds in this analogy), for a very large benefit to someone else in the future. This benefit is represented as the cash value or death benefit (other trees in this analogy), and then this organization could use this money anyway it wishes. This could be a lot of money. I feel that most people would like to give more than they do, but one reason they don't is because they feel they have to contribute large sums of money. We've all heard of big corporate donors and large foundations and what they can contribute, and we feel intimidated, but now you need not to be so. I will say, however, that there are many elaborate ways to use life insurance in this type of planning, but for brevity's sake, I will only go over some very basic and simple methods.

Two of the simplest ways to give is to make an organization an owner or a beneficiary of a life insurance policy you wish to purchase or on one you have already in force. If they are the owner, they can access any cash value they accumulate, or as a beneficiary, they will receive the death benefit. If you itemize deductions on your tax returns, you can deduct your premiums paid as a charitable deduction. You also will have the psychological peace of mind and good feeling that you know you have been able to give generously. The other simple way, at least conceptually, is that the owner of the policy can transact a life settlement transaction, and, of course, everything here is based on you as an insured. Please understand in any scenario involving life insurance for charitable giving, it would be your life as the life that is being insured.

Here Is a Simple Sample of One-Step Financial Success

Now, let's take a look at a sample situation to see how all of this could fit together. I am not going to be like everyone else and show you a real pie in the sky; this can only happen if the stars align right and penguins fly. This sample is what I feel can be a reasonably executable plan. There are many different scenarios that you can create. You, of course, are going to have to possess the discipline needed to execute this plan.

For this very plan, we will assume we have a husband and a wife both forty-six years old and in general good health. Now for the "good news." We will ask the husband to pay $1,389.93 per month and his wife to pay $1,018.38 per month. This policy will insure each person's life for $350,000. Now I will go over this again. I know that there are some of you who are saying, "This guy is fifteen eggs short of a dozen if he thinks he is going to expect a couple to pay almost $2,500 per month for any life insurance, let alone $350,000 worth each. For that amount of insurance, it should cost about $70 per month or maybe even $800 per month for the permanent policies you keep talking about." If you are one of these people with that sentiment, I understand, but you are looking at purchasing life insurance under the old paradigm, which is that life insurance is basically money going to someone else when I die, and there is little if any benefit for me while I'm alive. Let's try looking at it under the new paradigm, which is that this is a financial tool that will bring myself and my heirs financial security and freedom for the rest of our lives.

ONE-STEP FINANCIAL SUCCESS

As far as finding $2,500 per month premium is concerned, I want you to keep in mind that when I ask clients and perspective clients what percent of salary goes into their 401(k) plans, the vast majority will admit to investing 10 to 15% or more of this salary into these plans, and they don't even give it a second thought. But I will remind you again, this is a big no-no for reasons that we went over previously. Putting this in perspective, if the husband and wife in this example each earn $60,000 per year from their employer, they each would be contributing about $500 to $800 a month or more into their plan. My clients and prospective clients, again, wouldn't give much thought to doing this because it is a pretax contribution, meaning money taken out before it gets to you, and also, they are excited by the employer's 3% match. People also contribute money into these plans because they feel it this their only alternative and that this is what their company offers them, so they better take advantage of their employer's "generosity."

To make this plan work, you should obviously contribute less to your employer plan, and you would probably need about $900 a month extra each. You might have to cut down on the frappe drinks covered with mint drizzle and peach schnapps. The point is that this is your financial security we are talking about, and only you can make it happen. It simply comes down to how badly you want lifetime financial security.

Anyway, getting back to this example, with $2,500 per month during this time, the husband can access about $37,779, and the wife can access $33,382 yearly from this cash value for fifteen years once they reach age sixty-five. Please understand what this means. This means that each spouse can have their own pension of approximately $700 to $800 a week for fifteen years up to age eighty-one. That is like having a good paying job when you retire. But alas, like all good things, that must come to an end, but at age eighty-two, the wife will still have a cash surrender value of $166,693 and the death benefit of $516,693, and the husband will have the cash surrender value of $706,028 and the death benefit of $1,050,628. The death benefit for both is much more than the original death benefit and still at age eighty-two. This couple will have over $873,000 of cash surrender value for them while they are alive. I should say this is not terrible. If this couple had young children, no cash value would be counted adversely toward needs or academic-based financial aid qualification, and at that time, the aggregate cash surrender value of both plans are roughly $816,000.

Let us also assume that upon the death of the second spouse and over the years between, the first spouse's own qualified retirement plan earnings and the second spouse's inherited qualified retirement plan earnings totaled $1,200,000. The resulting tax liability would be approximately $444,000, and, certainly, the death benefit from the second spouse would be more than enough to pay these taxes. This is a type of financial security that you should want.

Now, it is time to turbocharge this couple's plan and also add another income stream to their retirement pot of gold. They can also use the cash value accumulated in their life insurance policy to fully satisfy and pay off their mortgage approximately ten years earlier. In this example, let us assume they had a mortgage debt on their home of $350,000 (the same amount as the original death benefit stated on their policies). This is a newly seasoned mortgage that charges 4% interest fixed over thirty years. As a result, their principal and interest payments every month totaled $1,670.95. If you remember, this couple was to start taking their systematic pension withdrawals of $50,000 a year from each of their policies. Before they start taking the withdrawals, both policies have an aggregate cash surrender value of $986,143. This mortgage that they are currently paying into will have a balance after twenty years of $165,040.17. For this couple, I would strongly suggest that for the first year only, not only should they start taking their withdrawals, but they should also withdraw the $165,040.17 between the two policies to fully satisfy their mortgage. I will ask you, "If they do not have to pay back the $1,670.95 per month principal and interest, who do you think gets to keep this money?" (Don't worry. This is not a trick question.) The answer is this couple.

Putting this altogether, not only does this couple receive a tax-free pension of approximately $700–800 per week for each spouse (or $71,100 per year). They also have an extra $1,670.95 per month smaller pension derived from the fact that they do not have to make these mortgage payments to the bank anymore. This is how you turn your household debt into retirement wealth. Stated another way, *you are turning your home into a lean, mean income stream machine.* Please note, however, that if a couple does exercise this option, they will have less cash value at the end of the time when the withdrawals would be taken. You also have to understand that sometimes you have to give up something to receive something.

This turbocharge option will work best if you have a newly or very early seasoned mortgage. Why? You need time for the insurance policy to build up enough cash value to be able to fully satisfy the mortgage balance. Also, this option will not work if you refinance your mortgage. Refinancing your mortgage will give to the bank all of the years that you will have paid into it. Essentially, you are starting over timewise. I have seen many homeowners get too cute and refinance their mortgage because they want to knock down their interest rate a half of a percent. Mortgage company advertising does not discourage people from refinancing. I wonder why. They advertise lower rates, quick approval, etc. Yes, it is possible that you can save a few hundred dollars, but they leave it up to you to figure out that in return for the small savings on your mortgage payment, your original thirty-year mortgage will become a thirty-five year, a forty-year, or longer mortgage. This is downright absurd! Brace yourself for a reprimand! *This is another example of why you should not listen to outside voices and you should follow your own head and heart to do what is right for you.* Okay, I'm done with that. Thank you.

These plans offer a great deal of flexibility. This couple could have requested a larger pension amount, a longer time to receive the pension, even a predetermined higher or lower death benefit, or change whatever variables they want with the period with these plans. Again, I cannot stress this enough: it is more important than ever to meet with a respected agent or planner to run a few scenarios with you. This is because of all the variables that we have discussed, you won't be able to get this type of counseling from an Internet site that sells policies or from a bank who offers life insurance because— and I say this rather respectfully—they will not have the skill set by and large to counsel you on this. They are bankers who make a living selling bank products like CDs, checking accounts, etc. "What's the catch?" is the most reasonable, most inevitable question I am asked. There is really no catch, although some people may not be able to qualify medically for the insurance, and as I mentioned before, this type of planning does not take a whole lot of financial expertise, but it requires time and discipline. This is not some "get rich quick" scheme or putting a large sum of money on number eighteen on the roulette wheel. For those that have the discipline needed, they will reap the rewards, just like in the above example.

One final thing I wish to say: for this example, I am using an index universal life policy. If you remember, I was lukewarm on its use. I still feel it is an excellent product, and this policy was able to showcase the points I wanted to bring out. If appropriate, by all means, this should be a type of policy to purchase. At the risk of annoying redundancy, I ask you to please use your due diligence.

I Love This Plan! But My Health Condition Could Be a Problem.

I will agree with you that this is a legitimate concern and one I will address now. I will also admit that some people, unfortunately, may not be afforded the opportunity to implement this plan because of health reasons. Now that I have said this, we are in an age of rapid advances in medical technologies. Insurance companies are slowly but surely embracing this fact and, as a result, are offering insurance to more people than they did in the past. Please understand that insurance companies in their most basic form are businesses. In that way, they are similar to your neighborhood dry cleaner or pizza parlor. They know they have to generate more revenue to keep the doors open. Revenue is generated in part by the collection of new premiums from sold policies. It is in their financial interest to offer insurance to anyone they reasonably can and not turn away anyone that asks for it.

Having said that, there is a lot of money at stake in the form of death benefit payments, and that is why insurance companies need to be conservative. It is imperative that you work closely with your agent or adviser, disclose everything about your health to him or her, and do not hold anything back no matter how big or small you think the problem is. Remember, your adviser is working with and not against you. A talented agent will always use his creative juices to find a solution that everyone will be happy with. Also, when you start the initial paperwork and go through the process of procuring the insurance, make sure that you disclose everything to the insurance company. The insurance companies generally want to see two things from you. They want good faith disclosure, and they want to see that you are taking the requisite steps needed to cure yourself or at least effectively manage your health condition. In simplest terms, that means they want to see that you are following your physician's advice and course of therapy. If the companies see this, then they would be more than willing to offer the insurance and work out something to make all parties happy. On the other hand, if you fail to disclose your health status and they find out about it themselves without your help or you are not taking care of yourself properly, then the insurance companies will get all hot, bothered, and extremely annoyed at you and will not be willing to offer anything.

I will tell you that the overwhelming vast majority of insurance companies will offer insurance for prospective clients who occasionally use marijuana recreationally. There is one major carrier (and in my opinion more will follow soon) that will evaluate the insurability risk of a prospective client who has been diagnosed as HIV-positive. Yes, I said a prospective client who has been diagnosed as HIV-positive. If this prospective client can meet a certain criterion, he or she will be offered insurance.

Earlier in the book, I had mentioned that one of the big advantages of a survivorship universal life policy is that someone with a health impairment can still be offered insurance. This could be another option for you. The point is that if you want this insurance, *don't stop trying until every avenue has been exhausted*. Put your adviser to work, and don't be afraid. You also have *me*. You can use me to answer any question you might have, or you can use me as you adviser or anything in between. I will show you how to contact me.

Foxes, Rabbits, and Humans

We are starting to get close to the end of our journey now, but I am reminded of this childhood fable that I think is very appropriate for the situation now—the childhood fable of the fox and the rabbit. The fox and the rabbit were walking in the woods, and they were talking about what they would do if a wolf came out to attack them. The rabbit meekly said he would run into a hole and hide until the wolf disappeared. The fox laughed and said, "Is that all you can do?" The fox continues, "I could run away or climb a tree and ambush him or..." Just then, a wolf came after them. The rabbit, true to his word, ran into a hole. The fox stood frozen. He wasn't sure which option to take. While he stood there thinking, the wolf pounced on him and had fox with fries for lunch.

Here is the point. We will all have reasons to not to investigate this new alternative way of investing and planning without the 401(k) plans or stock plans or whatever. Different things demand our financial attention. Other people will probably discourage you from investigating this method. (They probably have not done any investing like this themselves either.) Don't be like the fox and procrastinate. Be like the rabbit and take immediate action. Remember, the rabbit did not have some elaborate, stylish plan. He just had a plan that would work. Now you have one also.

Remember, your employer does not care what you do in terms of saving for your post-employment future. Our government certainly hopes you do nothing. Remember this. Only you can take care of you and your family's financial future. Please allow yourself the freedom to explore this out-of-the-box method of investing and legacy planning. Either I, or another respected agent, or adviser will help you run the numbers and advise you if this method is right for you. There will be no pressure and no hassle. I have learned that in our skeptical society of today, any attempt of applying this type of pressure will cause you to run for the hills. Even if we never meet personally, I do sincerely hope you investigate this, and if you feel that this is the right type of planning that you should be doing, then you should be executing this type of plan for your financial security.

Conclusion and Final Thoughts

Okay, we are almost at the point where you can get rid of me. (I mean the end of the book.) Now you know how to achieve what we are calling one-step financial success, but I want to explain what is the worst mistake you can make in your general financial planning. If you remember, I told you what the second worst mistake is. I know this is going to sound odd, but in my opinion, it is also the worst mistake we make. This mistake is that is we listen to many other people or voices telling us what to do. We also use current events to guide us to make our own decisions. Seriously, why should our trade wars with China, the Middle East crisis, Brexit, or any other outside event determine our financial success or failure? I know that you know by now that you need not worry about your external environment if you implement the one-step financial success method we have spoken about.

There is just one more personal story that I need to share. I am saving this for the end because I wrestled with the idea of putting this in the book in the first place. In 1992, I was very young and green, both in my professional life and personal life. I was born in December, so I was always young for my age. I started the financial services business right after graduation from college. I was twenty-two years old when I started. Naturally, I was still learning and making my mistakes. I started working with this husband and wife client very early in the year. They had purchased large-amount term policies to pay off a mortgage if one of the spouses died. Each spouse took $300,000 of insurance, and this couple was young, and this premium was very low. About five months later, another adviser who I perceived to have had an existing relationship with these people started working with them. I assume this adviser did not speak highly of the work I had done for this client and I guess told them that I was not someone to work with. My clients called me angrily to explain that they no longer wished to keep the insurance I had sold them, and they explained about what the other adviser had said about me. In a situation like that, it is hard to defend yourself, and I was not able to do so very well, and finally, I probably was not as aggressive as I probably should have been in defending myself. Possibly, because of guilt that I had done a horrible job for these clients. Fast-forward about seven months, and that brings us to February of 1993. I am from New York City, as you know, and if you recall, that was when the first terrorist attack on the World Trade Center towers took place. The husband client was one of the people who perished on that horrific day. There were only six people to do so. He was an employee of one of the ground-level restaurants in the tower that was attacked and was buried in the rubble. I was heartbroken and literally in a daze for about a month, maybe longer. Obviously, to this day, I am guilty and angry at myself for not doing more for these clients. I felt guilty for not doing more even though he listened to someone else about not keeping his insurance, and they made their own decision.

This is why I have been harping on the fact that you have to shut out all of the noise and make decisions based on what you feel you should do logically or emotionally. I guess that these clients did not replace my insurance with anything else. I had learned that the wife and children did receive substantial charitable donations. I knew that Prudential insurance company, whom I was with at the time as a captive agent, would not pay this family the $300,000 that they would have needed to pay off the mortgage in full. I will drive around and see the home in Brooklyn, NY, all boarded and unlivable. I knew it would be hard for this family because English was not their first language, although they did speak English quite well. And they originally were not from the United States. I surmised that the wife and children left and went back to their own country. I felt that this day was the day I received my professional big boy pants, and I realized that it was my duty to make sure that if a client wanted to decide about their financial future, that they understood the consequences and they acted on their own accord.

ONE-STEP FINANCIAL SUCCESS

One-Step Financial Success has been a culmination of almost thirty years of work in the financial services industry, and it's been my privilege and honor to put this pen to paper to help everyone I can to achieve the financial security we all need and deserve. Even if we never meet personally, please know that there is a pesky blonde insurance guy type from Long Island, NY, who is rooting for you when times are tough, and it feels that everything is against you, and then you might have difficulty at times implementing this plan. I am not promising it to be easy, but I am promising it will be richly rewarding at the end. I hope that the dominant thoughts in your mind from now on will not be about monetary worries but of peace, love, and leaving a legacy to your fellow man. So long for now.

Acknowledgments

Putting together a self-help book like this is a labor of love, but this could not have been done by myself. I needed the help of many people to put this together, and I will acknowledge as many people as I can. I do apologize in advance for any omissions.

To my literary agent, Mr. Robert Germann; my publishing coordinator, Trevor Boyd; Mr. Dustin Robert, the corporate president; and the rest of the Page Publishing staff, thank you for believing in me, being patient with me, and sticking by me through this long process that involved many delays. I do thank the staff of Page Publishing for being the champion of *One-Step Financial Success* and believing that it can touch the world positively.

To my daughter, Carmela, you are a rock star. You are my gifted, multi-talented millennial who is mature way beyond her eleven years of existence. Without your general support and specially technical expertise in helping me put together *One-Step Financial Success*, the thoughts that I have put down on this paper would've just remained as thoughts in my head, not to be shared with the rest of the world on paper. To Carmela, I appreciate all of your hard work in helping me put together this book. And I thank you for being the wonderful daughter that you are, and know that I will always be proud of you. Also, I want to thank you for actually suggesting the title for the book.

To my son, Barnard "Barney," who has been diagnosed with autism, I am your biggest fan. You give me inspiration when things get tough to go on and keep working. I am proud of the progress you are making in overcoming your autism and curing yourself. You have come a long way, and I am proud of you, and thank you for providing the family with your happiness, love, and joy.

To my mother, Cynthia, who, although she is not with us anymore, will always be an inspiration to me and always has been an inspiration to me. My mother was a single parent trying to raise four boys by herself with no help and limited financial means. I still don't know where she got the strength to do this, but she was able to do that. My mother also gave me the gift of being able to clearly express my words in writing. Without the gift of writing confidence, I could not even remotely think of putting a book like this together. With that, I thank you, Mom, and I will love you always.

To my lovely wife, Michele, I owe you a debt I know that I can never repay, but I want to acknowledge all the love and support you have given me. You are a perfect wife and mother. You seem to know when to be tough, funny, kind, and supportive when you feel you need to be. I know that it is all to make me the best husband and father I can be. I don't know how you put up with me sometimes. You have not always agreed with my actions. And I know that you've had to endure a lot of painful years because of my struggling, but I do want you to know that I love you always, and your love is something that I always will treasure every day of my life. I will always try to be the best husband and father that I possibly can be. So, to you, please accept my eternal love and gratitude. And also know without you and your love, I could not even conceive of a dream like this, of putting a book like this together.

Lastly, I want to acknowledge all of my clients and prospective clients. A good many of you have become personal friends of mine as well, and for that I will always be grateful for. But all of you have each contributed to my experience and expertise level in some way. And I would like to would like to think that this book is basically a compilation of all the experiences that I have built up in working with all of you. Again, I wish all of you the best in your financial life, and to all of you, I wish you the best in all of your life's undertakings.

Notes

Coakley, Emily "1997: Bodies of Heaven's Gate Cult Members Discovered After Mass Suicide", Dated August 15, 2018: 2daysearch.com/1997-bodies-of-heavens-gate-cult-members-discovered-after-mass-suicide/.

Joseph, Evelyn: Opening Heavens Gate, "How 39 Believers Ascended to Heaven in UFO's": Dated September 24, 2017: STMUhistorymedia.org/opening-heavens-gate.

The Institute for College Access and Success: Press release dated September 18, 2018. "Class of 2017 Four Year Graduates' Average Student Debt is $28,650": https://ticas.org/affordability-2/class2017-four-year-graduates-average-student-debt-28650/.

The Week magazine "Business: The News at A Glance: The Bottom Line" p.30 left side, dated February 3, 2012, Business Editor Collingwood, Harris.

The Institute for College Access and Success: Press release dated September 18, 2018. "Class of 2017 Four Year Graduates' Average Student Debt is $28,650": https://ticas.org/affordability-2/class2017-four-year-graduates-average-student-debt-28650/.

Erin Duffin, "Share of Old Age Population (65 Years and Older) in the Total US Population from 1950 to 2050," https://www.statista.com/statistics/457822/share-of-old-age-population-in-the-total-us-population.

"Federal Debt Clock," US Government Spending, https://www.usgovernmentdebt.us.

Amir El-Sibaie, "2019 Tax Brackets," Tax Foundation, https://taxfoundation.org/2019-tax-brackets/.

"Federal Estate Tax Exemptions 1997 through 2019," The Balance, https://thebalance.com/exemption-from-federal-estate-taxes 1916-1997-3505636.

LongTermCare.gov: (managed by the US Department of Health and Human services): "How Much Care Will You Need?" https://longtermcare.aci.gov/the basics/how-much-care-will-you-need.html.

American Benefits Council: American Benefits Council 401(k) fast facts table dated January, 2019: www.americanbenefitscouncil.org; From table of Current Defined Contribution Plan Data based on 2016 Form 5500 Annual Reports, released December, 2018. Total assets column.

Ameritas Life Insurance Corp. of New York Excel Plus Index Universal Life's proposed insureds are male and female, both forty-six years old. The insurance is issued at standard nontobacco rates, nonguaranteed current interest rate earning 6.80%, assuming gross annual withdrawals of $50,000 each. The male is insured an annual premium of $16,679, and the female is insured an annual premium of $12,221.

https://www.bankrate.com/calculators/mortgages/amortization-calculator.aspx P.13 from amortization schedule obtained after populating mortgage calculator with the following data $350,000 price of home, 30 years, 4% interest: balance number on the September 2039 line.

About the Author

Mark A. Schlossberg, CLU, is the founder and president of MAS Financial Solutions. He has been assisting clients with the execution of their financial plans for over twenty-nine years. He started his career with Prudential Financial as one of their representatives immediately after receiving his bachelor of arts degree from Brooklyn College of the City University of New York. He founded MAS Financial Solutions with the idea of offering present and future clients more alternatives to help them implement their plans. His work has financially enhanced the lives of thousands of clients worldwide. His objective is to enable clients to achieve financial security and success without having to worry about outside factors and events but to only worry about taking action to execute the steps they need to take to achieve financial success. This is the inspiration for *One-Step Financial Success*. He has earned the chartered life underwriter (or CLU) designation. The CLU Designation is awarded by The American College, Bryn Mawr, Pennsylvania. This is one of the most prestigious designations in the financial services industry. He lives in Long Island, New York, with his wife and two children. He can be reached at masfinancialsolutions@gmail.com.